THE TWENTIES

Text by Martha Saxton
Edited by Jeffrey Weiss

The publishers wish to thank the following for permission to reprint illustrations in this book: Wide World Photos, pp. 7, 14, 15, 16, 17, 21, 26, 27, 28; New York Public Library, pp. 8, 29; Ford News Department, pp. 10-11; UPI, pp. 4-5, 12-13, 20, 25, 30; International Newsreel, pp. 18, 22-23, 24; Columbia Records, p. 32; KDKA Radio, p. 19.

Book and cover design by Mark Stein

Music compiled by Gordon Williams

Photo research by Judy Hinger

Printed in the United States of America.

International Standard Book Number: 0-8256-4197-7
Library of Congress Catalog Card Number: 75-32890

CONTENTS

THE TWENTIES

Suffragettes celebrating victory, Aug. 31, 1920.

THE HARDING FOLLIES

Warren G. Harding, second-rate senator from Ohio, appeared to be just what the country wanted after the rigor and high-mindedness of the Great War as conducted by Woodrow Wilson. Whereas Wilson can be described with some accuracy as a tragedy, Harding, with equal accuracy, can be considered a travesty. A weak, handsome man with a shortage in the brains department, Harding might have escaped from the presidency unscathed were it not for the help of his friends.

Harding's first major contribution to the United States came in the form of a neologism. In 1920, during his campaign, Harding summed up America's desires. "America's present need is not heroism but healing, not nostrums but normalcy, not revolution but restoration . . . not surgery but serenity." In addition to "normalcy," Harding contributed "bloviate," a verb which described his addiction to the sound of his own voice. Former Secretary of the Treasury William Gibbs McAdoo said that listening to Harding gave him "the impression of an army of pompous phrases moving over the landscape in search of an idea."

Harding moved into the White House on March 4, 1921, complete with his sour, ambitious wife and his all-American dog, Laddie Boy. A friendly, affable man, he impressed everyone with his openness, accessibility and limited capacity for understanding. William Allen White recalled the President coming out of the office of an aide saying, "John, I can't make a damn thing out of this tax problem. I listen to one side and they seem right, and then–God! I talk to the other side and they seem just as right, and here I am where I started. I know somewhere there is a book that will give me the truth, but, hell, I couldn't read the book. I know somewhere there is an economist who knows the truth, but I don't know where to find him and haven't the sense to know him and trust him when I find him. God! What a job!"

Harding's major nonlinguistic contribution to the country was the legend of Teapot Dome, a scandal which required fifty years to top. The President made a number of foolish appointments, including that of his brother-in-law as Superintendent of Prisons; but most foolish of all were those of Albert B. Fall as Secretary of the Interior and Harry Daugherty as Attorney General. Early in the administration the two made the acquaintance of Teapot Dome, Wyoming, government land with oil on it which was being held in reserve for the future needs of the Navy. In 1920 this oil was about to be unavoidably siphoned off by neighboring wells. To forestall this, Congress gave the Secretary of the Navy power to deal with the problem. He decided to have wells drilled along the periphery of the deposit to prevent drainage. When Fall entered the cabinet he got Harding to sign an order delivering the disposition of the reserves over to him. Fall subsequently authorized his dear friend Harry F. Sinclair of Mammoth Oil Company exclusive rights to drill the oil. There was, of course, no competitive bidding on this or either of the other two reserves in question. In return Sinclair bestowed upon the generous Fall some $260,000 in Liberty bonds.

The President, meanwhile, was occupied playing poker, drinking and arranging meetings with his mistress, Nan Britton. Nan was to become the author of *The President's Daughter*, a very popular book in which she revealed some of the scrapes in which she and Warren found themselves. Their child, she believed, had been conceived in a coat closet in the White House. They were once broken in on by private detectives in a New York hotel, but Harding had told Nan that everything was all right since he was traveling in his capacity as a senator "en route to Washington to serve the people."

Harding left in the summer of 1923 for an extended visit to Alaska. He had many friends on his mind. Throughout the trip, according to William Allen White, "he kept asking Secretary Hoover and the more trusted reporters who surrounded him what a President should do whose friends had betrayed him." Coming home Harding got sick and suddenly died in San Francisco on August 2, 1923. The official cause of death is still uncertain, and there was speculation about suicide and even murder. Mrs. Harding seemed like a possible suspect, whose motive would have been jealousy of Nan. In any case, Harding was well out of it when the fumes from the Teapot Dome began to rise.

President and Mrs. Harding, July 4, 1923.

Clara Bo

FLAPPER

Woman Suffrage became a congressional fact in 1919 when the amendment was sent to the states. Conventional wisdom had it that the amendment made no difference, that elections were unchanged by the new voters. The new voters, however, were changing in a sexual and social revolution which was far more important than a piece of legislation ever could be.

"David and Alabama kicked over the oak leaves from the stumpy roots in the woods and picked white violets. They went on Sundays to the vaudeville and sat in the back of the theatre so they could hold hands unobserved. They learned to sing "My Sweetie" and "Baby" and sat in a box at *Hitchy-Koo* and gazed at each other soberly through the chorus of "How Can You Tell?" The spring rains soaked through the heavens till the clouds slid open and summer flooded the South with sweat and heat waves. Alabama dressed in pink and pale linen and she and David sat together under the paddles of ceiling fans whipping the summer to consequence." So reads the languid prose of Zelda Sayre Fitzgerald in her autobiographical novel *Save Me the Waltz*. Zelda was a southern belle turned flapper—spoiled, beautiful, capricious, perverse, risqué, given to unpredictable antics, shocking escapades, drinking from hip flasks in roadsters. Zelda got tipsy, rolled her stockings down, threw away her corset (indeed, all her clothes on occasion), danced close, necked, passed from beau to beau, bobbed her hair and said unladylike things.

The revolution of the twenties, which seems tame now, was cataclysmic at the time. It affected a whole generation, not just a few intellectuals and dissidents. Sex was on everyone's mind. Horrifyingly simplified, Freud traveled through cocktail parties and out into the cars going home. People had complexes and libidos and sex was the answer. Sex was also the question—how far, how much, with whom, when, where?

Sex was It as Elinor Glyn put it in her novel of the same name. Ms. Glyn announced that in all of Hollywood only Clara Bow qualified as the "It" girl. "To have 'It'," she wrote, "the fortunate possessor must have that strange magnetism which attracts both sexes. There must be physical attraction, but beauty is unnecessary." Clara, lovely girl from Brooklyn, became "The Hottest Jazz Baby in Films." Not a brilliant girl, Clara attributed her success as the world's most desirable flapper to her ability to give complete attention in conversation. Sex it was, however, and it was igniting the Flaming Youth and incensing their parents.

Rich Episcopal ladies like Mrs. J. Pierpont Morgan, Mrs. James Roosevelt and Mrs. Borden Harriman got together to discuss ways to prevent "improper ways of dancing" and "excess of nudity." A Dress Reform Committee sprang up in Philadelphia to design the "moral gown." Ministers of fifteen denominations were canvassed and the result was a very moral item, loose-fitting, with long sleeves and a skirt that was only and exactly seven and a half inches off the floor. It should come as no surprise that the moral gown wasn't a big hit in New York. State legislatures, worried about what was happening to their women, decided to repair their defective morals. Utah had plans to fine women with skirts "higher than three inches above the ankle." In Virginia they were worried about dresses displaying "more than three inches of throat." In Ohio the limit was two inches of throat and other regulations included prohibition of the sale of any "garment which unduly displays or accentuates the lines of the female figure." And further they would prevent any "female over fourteen years of age" from wearing "a skirt which does not reach to that part of the foot known as the instep."

The legislators could legislate and fulminate *ad nauseam* but things were permanently changed. F. Scott Fitzgerald's *This Side of Paradise* came out in 1920 and explained to parents that their daughters were kissing, necking and petting, and worst of all, *talking* about what they were doing with a cynicism which seemed masculine. They had jumped off their own pedestals and were gleefully kicking them over.

"Gillespie: I love you.

"Rosalind (Coldly): I know it.

"Gillespie: And you haven't kissed me for two weeks. I had an idea that after a girl was kissed she was—was—won.

"Rosalind: Those days are over. I have to be won all over again every time you see me.

"Gillespie: Are you serious?

"Rosalind: About as usual. There used to be two kinds of kisses: first when girls were kissed and deserted; second, when they were engaged. Now there's a third kind, when the man is kissed and deserted. If Mr. Jones of the nineties bragged he'd kissed a girl, everyone knew he was through with her. If Mr. Jones of 1919 brags the same everyone knows it's because he can't kiss her anymore. Given a decent start any girl can beat a man nowadays.

"Gillespie: Then why do you play with men?

"Rosalind (Leaning forward confidentially): For that first moment, when he's interested. There is a moment—oh, just before the first kiss, a whispered word—something that makes it worthwhile."

Clara Bow.

CARS

If the decade deserves to be called "roaring" it is because of the automobile industry which came of age in those years. Car ownership soared (or roared) from six million to twenty-three million by the end of the period. The car was suddenly the single most popular and important commodity in the United States. Nothing has changed this country as much as the relative cheapness, availability and popularity of the automobile. The car renovated cities, courtship, vacations, families, concepts of time and distance—concepts, in short, of the possible.

Physically, cars changed enormously between 1919 and 1929. Only ten percent had been closed at the beginning of the decade, and by the end only ten percent were open. Manufacturers offered new, sleek styling, low bodies, balloon tires and an array of jazzy colors. Even Henry Ford had to change his design. In 1927, after a $1,300,000 publicity campaign, Ford revealed the Model A, his first change since his originality and genius had produced the Model T. More than a million people came to look at the new car and many lingered to buy. New automobile design was considered in the same category as a scientific invention or the cure for a disease.

Other cars, by manufacturers who have long since vanished, were also popular. The Jordan Playboy, for example, a luxury car designed by Ned Jordan, was manufactured in small quantities for rich people. Jordan, who instituted a then unique advertising campaign to sell the car, said, "We *did* make a lot of money *awfully* fast." Jordan's ads, entitled "Somewhere West of Laramie," featured a hazy drawing of a woman driving a dreamy car, followed by a precursor of the Marlboro man riding alongside full tilt on his horse. The gist of the copy was that somewhere out there was a girl romantic enough, tough (but vulnerable) enough, beautiful, sexy, saucy, independent, tanned and rich as hell, whose life would be made complete by owning a Jordan Playboy. The ad was a kind of challenge to see if you could handle a car as spirited, exotic and luxurious as a Playboy. There was, in the copy, no mention of spark plugs, carburetors or any of the other grimy realities of cars which permeated more straightforward (and less successful) advertising.

Another opportunity for luxurious driving was the Lincoln, not remodeled every year because, as the ad said, "it would be unjust in the extreme to subject Lincoln owners to that artificial and wasteful depreciation." Lincolns were designed to duplicate lavish coaches of the nineteenth century. Even the Lincoln copywriters seemed out of the nineteenth century. "Emblematic of the days when the gentry of England and America found enjoyment in travel behind prancing horses, this coaching brougham commands immediate interest. Old-world picturesqueness lives anew. English coaching colors enliven the exterior. The interior is a true reproduction of the early Concord coaches." And then there was the Cadillac arm of General Motors which produced, for the well-heeled, the Sport Phaeton, a racy car promoted in hushed tones more appropriate to a church than a car ad. "Forms crumble. Motion finally comes to rest. Sound sinks to silence. Color alone abides. Here, in a rose resplendent in June sunlight; in the lavender shadows on January snows; in the adamantine heart of a gem buried deep in

Clad in fur coat and derby hat, a couple motor through the woods in a 1920 Ford Model T Roadster.

the core of earth—Nature hangs her earth with rich tapestries." That not being enough, the unhinged brochurist continues, "In the automotive world, it is not enough that cars be colorful. They should be colored as Nature paints. The deep green of the forest is peaceful, cheerful, refreshing. It invites to relaxation, to whole-souled enjoyment of the hour." This, of course, pertained to the green of the Sport Phaeton, complete with two folding windshields and a searchlight "mounted on a nickeled stanchion on the right running board."

So, the Ford Model T gave way to an abundance of cars, improved, faster, more comfortable and reliable. It was during the twenties that the American addiction to automobiles became irrevocable.

PROHIBITION

The Eighteenth Amendment was ratified and went into effect on January 16, 1920. The Amendment was supported by the National Prohibition Act or the Volstead Act, named for its creator, a bill which was to implement the Amendment and render the United States of America dry—also God-fearing, reverent, thrifty, punctual, mannerly, and clean behind the ears. Prohibition certainly had less success as a reform measure and more violent and startling repercussions than anything the Anti-Saloon League or the Women's Christian Temperance Union could have imagined, much less predicted.

The Anti-Saloon League issued a statement the day before Prohibition took effect. "At one minute past twelve tomorrow morning a new nation will be born . . . Now for an era of clear thinking and clean living!" William Jennings Bryan at his sixtieth birthday party two months later announced that the liquor issue was "as dead as slavery." The first Prohibition Commissioner, John F. Kramer, got a little out of hand in his oracular predictions. "This law will be obeyed in cities, large and small, and in villages, and where it is not obeyed it will be enforced . . . The law says that liquor to be used as a beverage must not be manufactured. We shall see that it is not manufactured. Nor sold, nor given away, nor hauled in anything on the surface of the earth or under the earth or in the air." Poor Commissioner Kramer was in for a nasty shock. In a piece of shortsightedness which he could not have avoided, Daniel C. Roper, Commissioner of Internal Revenue, predicted: "The Prohibition law will be violated—extensively at first, slightly later on; but it will, broadly speaking, be enforced and will result in a nation that knows not alcohol." As it turned out, of course, the nation didn't know a great many things, but one of them was not alcohol. And, it turned out, that however badly the Wets had been organized, and they had failed miserably in preventing Prohibition, they were to succeed brilliantly in circumventing it.

Home stills, cocktail parties, hip flasks—drinking, its paraphernalia, vocabulary and rituals positively *flourished* in the twenties. People became ingenious liquor brewers and many tasted liquors never brewed before or after. Senator Morris of Texas, who wrote the Eighteenth Amendment, was discovered to have a still producing 130 gallons of whisky a day on his property. California winegrowers developed a grape juice called Vin-Glo which, when tended to for sixty days, turned into fifteen percent alcohol by volume wine. Beer was illegal, but near-beer, or one-half of one

Al Capone

percent alcohol, wasn't. The stuff was pretty unpopular, but brewers like Pabst discovered that if they made it without alcohol and sold it with a package of yeast to complete the process, they would be selling do-it-yourself beer. And a New York winegrower devised a grape product which resembled a pound of butter. The directions sternly advised against adding water or wine would result. Doctors could prescribe alcohol for medicinal purposes, and during Prohibition the medicinal uses of booze grew to a million gallons a year. The Federal authorities didn't even try to prevent this practice.

Fiorello La Guardia suggested that 250,000 policemen were needed to enforce Prohibition in New York City alone. And another 200,000 to patrol the patrolmen. Instead, in 1920, the entire country had 1,520 brave men standing between it and delirium tremens. By 1930, when the problem had been demonstrated in no uncertain terms on the streets of Chicago, New York and Detroit, in speakeasies and stills across the nation, the Feds provided 2,836 men who were paid the bribably-low salary of $2,800 a year, maximum.

Prohibition, since it was not to be obeyed, required risk-takers seeking high profits to get alcohol from its source into the highball glasses of the Wets. George Remus was one of the more likable purveyors of liquor the twenties produced. He was a Chicago lawyer with some pharmaceutical training, which stood him in good stead when he decided to make medicinal alcohol. He bought many distilleries and hired 3,000 men to steal his produce. In a very few years he was worth five million dollars which he spent with unique abandon. Like Chicago gangster Dion O'Bannion and Ferdinand the Bull, Remus fancied flowers and surrounded himself with them indoors and out. He gave parties at which guests could expect to receive $100-bills, cars and jewels. He had a 60 by 20 foot swimming pool of Italian marble installed and set about with hundreds of plants. He had a gold piano. He also had a wife named Imogene whom he shot and killed when he discovered that she was fooling around with the Fed who had fingered him and sent him to prison for nineteen months. Remus was acquitted of her murder on the grounds of temporary insanity, although his house could not be so easily excused.

Chicago, of course, was notorious for Prohibition violence, largely because Johnny Torrio, while setting up his bootlegging establishment, decided he needed help and called one Alphonse Capone, a twenty-three-year-old New Yorker, out to Chicago to help him.

Barrels of beer emptied into Lake Michigan by federal agents.

Capone quickly gathered a small army of 700 men skilled in the art of sawed-off shotgunnery. By 1925 Capone controlled the suburb of Cicero, owned its mayor and was ruler of its gambling casinos and all 161 of its bars. He no longer needed Torrio.

Chicago's other gangs presented Capone with few problems. Florist and orchid fancier Dion O'Bannion died in his flower shop, shot by three of Capone's men. Capone, always a stylist, sent a large floral arrangement to Dion's funeral with a tag "From Al." Capone disposed of the rest of the O'Bannions on St. Valentine's Day, 1929. Three of his men, dressed as policemen, walked into the O'Bannion garage where seven gangsters were waiting for a delivery of liquor. The bogus cops ordered the O'Bannions to disarm and line up. The O'Bannions, not fearing Chicago's finest, complied and were promptly shot to death by two more men in street clothes. The police impersonators then marched the killers away and all five, of course, escaped.

Capone, who professed to know nothing of such incidents, made a point about hypocrisy when he quarreled with the nation's verbal niceties. "Everybody calls me a racketeer. I call myself a businessman. When I sell liquor it's bootlegging. When my patrons serve it on a silver tray on Lake Shore Drive, it's hospitality."

VALENTINO

Rudolf Alfonzo Raffaele Pierre Filibert Gugliemi di Valentina d'Antonguollo was his real name, otherwise known as "The Sheik." He came to this country from Italy in 1913 when he was eighteen. He had no particular skills but a fondness for gardening and an enthusiasm for dancing. He danced well enough to be invited to perform at Maxim's, a job which in turn got him a road tour, which took him all the way to Hollywood. There he was persuaded by director Emmett Flynn to try his hand (or, in Valentino's case, his eyes) at movies. The young man agreed and made his first important film (*The Four Horsemen of the Apocalypse*) in 1921. His role was a highborn, high-spirited South American who goes to fight for France in the Great War. Valentino was not a star overnight and made a number of dismal pictures until he moved from Metro to Paramount for $500 a week. They immediately slapped him into *The Sheik*, which turned him into the definitive lover.

It wasn't so much that Valentino had talent, although he did have natural grace, athletic ability, and a genuine and obvious sweetness, but he did possess more of It than any male performer in Hollywood. "Catnip to women," H. L. Mencken said. He bugged his eyes out, flared his nostrils and clenched his jaw with an intensity and apparent passion which stirred the blood of his women fans. None of his films was artistically memorable—*Moran of the Lady Letty, Blood and Sand, Monsieur Beaucaire, Cobra, Beyond the Rocks, The Eagle* and finally, *Son of the Sheik*—but each was, in its way, an event.

In August 1926, Valentino was in New York promoting *Son of the Sheik* when he became very ill and was taken to the Polyclinic Hospital for a gallstone operation. It appeared that he was getting better when suddenly, on August 23, he died. Mark Hellinger summed it up in vivid Hollywoodese, "Rudolph Valentino, the man who brought happiness to the hearts of millions, is dead. The Great Director, who plays no favorites in screening the scenario of life, took him away at 12:10 p.m. yesterday."

Valentino's death was as spectacular and rather more profitable than his life. Harry C. Klemfuss, Valentino's manager, choreographed the star's funeral so that mourners lined up for eleven blocks around the bier supplied by New York undertaker to the stars, Frank E. Campbell. Klemfuss provided the press with photographs of the funeral cortège, posed in advance so that the papers wouldn't have to wait for the real thing, and information on the undertaker's establishment. The hysteria generated by the event was international. In London a dancer poisoned herself and a New York woman, thorough if inefficient, swallowed iodine and shot herself twice before she finally collapsed onto a heap of Valentino photographs.

New York tabloids made capital from Valentino's demise by inventing a story in which the actor had died from a dose of arsenic administered for motives of revenge or jealousy. Pola Negri, papers reported, fainted when she heard the news about Valentino. She appeared at the funeral supported by companions and disclosed that she and the dead man had been planning to marry. Ultimately 100,000 mourned publicly for Valentino and 75 to 100 people were injured in the crowd grieving for this unexpected casualty.

The publicity attendant on the funeral put Valentino's estate in the black by $600,000, his manager reported. And the word "sheik," meaning a young lover, male variety, companion of a flapper or "sheba," entered the vocabulary.

LUCKY LINDY

"Lucky" was a name the slender, six-foot-three pilot, known to his friends as "Slim," always hated. And it was inapt, since Lindbergh's flight had little to do with luck and a great deal to do with courage, confidence and good planning.

Charles Augustus Lindbergh, Jr., son of Evangeline Land and Charles Augustus Lindbergh, was born in Detroit in 1902. His father was a Congressman, and seventeen years older than his wife, a shy, reserved woman who disliked her husband's career. The Lindberghs unofficially separated when Charles was a little boy, and he went to live with his mother, an inveterate traveler. After two years at the University of Wisconsin, Lindbergh enrolled at the Nebraska Aircraft Corporation. "Slim" paid $500 to learn his trade.

Shortly he was barnstorming, wing walking, and jumping with a new invention, the parachute. By 1926, Lindbergh was planning his historic transatlantic trip. He had recently encountered a new, expensive, light, flexible, durable plane, the Wright-Bellanca monoplane. "Judging from the accounts I've read, (the Bellanca) is the most efficient plane ever built. It could break the world's endurance record, and the transcontinental, and set a dozen marks for range and speed and weight. Possibly—my mind is startled at its thought—" he wrote in his autobiography, "I could fly nonstop between New York and Paris."

Raymond Orteig, a French-born hotel owner, offered, in 1919 and again in 1924, $25,000 for the first nonstop flight between France and New York. Lindbergh's problem was getting a plane. He managed to find backers to stand him to the price which he put together with a young designer who eventually built the Spirit of St. Louis for him.

It remained only to make the flight. After a brief visit from his mother on the 14th of May, 1927, who said economically, "Goodbye Charles. And luck," Slim sat back to wait for the weather to give him his chance. At 7:52 a.m., May 20, he took off from Roosevelt Field, first uncertainly, gradually gaining confidence as he gained altitude. He had not slept for twenty-four hours and had thirty-four sleepless ones ahead of him. He struggled with ice, clouds, turbulence, fog, and most of all, his desire to sleep, when, finally and miraculously, he landed in Le Bourget, the Paris airfield, at 10:22 p.m. Paris time on May 21, to be surrounded by an hysterical crowd of French enthusiasts. Lindbergh was completely unprepared for his welcome. "When I circled the aerodrome it did not occur to me that any connection existed between me and my arrival and the

This page: Rudolph Valentino and Pola Negri. *Opposite page*: Colonel Charles Lindbergh and Mrs. Lomar Oliver, Jr. Roosevelt Field, Long Island, May 13, 1927.

cars stalled in traffic on the roads," he wrote. "When my wheels touched earth I had no way of knowing that tens of thousands of men and women were breaking down fences and flooding past guards." The mob at Le Bourget would have made off with Lindbergh had not two French pilots removed his helmet and placed it on the head of a tall Frenchman, diverting the attention of the well-wishers.

Despite Lindbergh's exhaustion, he was polite, poised and a charming hero whom the French loved and Americans were preparing to canonize. Coolidge sent the cruiser *Memphis* to retrieve Lindbergh and his plane, the two of them arriving on June 11, to be met by fifty planes roaring over the ship. Coolidge and Mrs. Lindbergh came aboard and Fitzhugh Green wrote of the laconic President's welcome, "Those closest to Mr. Coolidge say that rarely has he shown the unrestrained cordiality he put into that single greeting." There followed dinners, parades, more than 55,000 telegrams (one was 520 feet long with 17,500 signatures), tickertape, the Distinguished Flying Cross, the Congressional Medal of Honor, offers of two and a half million dollars for an air tour, $700,000 to appear in the movies. Lindbergh had, as the National Press Club put it, reinstated "clean living, clean thinking, fair play and sportsmanship, modesty of speech and manner, faith in a mother's prayers" by proving that these qualities "have a front-page news value." For a nation which was in deep need of heroes, Lindbergh did a good and creditable job.

Jack Dempsey in training at Saratoga Lake, New York, July 1927.

SPORTS HEROES

Babe Ruth, 1923.

People devoured sports in the twenties with a brand-new appetite—batting averages, yards gained, meters swum, balls caught, services broken, birdies shot. In the search for heroes, Jack Dempsey turned up, and when he fought the aging Georges Carpentier in 1921 in Jersey City, the fight earned over one and a half million dollars from more than 75,000 enthusiastic fans. Carpentier went down in the fourth round, and Dempsey held on to his title. Two years later he successfully defended it against Argentina's Luis Firpo. Dempsey, who had won the crown in 1919 from Jess Willard, suffered his first loss by decision at the gloves of young Shakespeare-quoting Gene Tunney. Dempsey couldn't believe he had lost. "What happened?" asked his wife. "Honey," Dempsey replied, "I forgot to duck." He promptly challenged Tunney to a rematch. That fight took place in Chicago's Soldier Field. It looked as if Dempsey had won—Tunney went down but the referee was slow beginning the count, partly because Dempsey hadn't retired to a neutral corner. So, Tunney got a total of thirteen precious seconds to recover himself. That he did and spent the rest of the fight moving away from the exhausted older man, who never regained his title. Tunney, a man of many interests, only held the title a year when he quit to go on a European walking tour with Thornton Wilder, lecture on Shakespeare and marry a Greenwich, Connecticut, lady. Tunney wasn't a graceful writer or lecturer, but he was trying, as his statement on returning to America demonstrates: "It is hard to realize as our ship passes through the Narrows that fifteen months have elapsed since the *Mauretania* was carrying me in the other direction. During those fifteen months Mrs. Tunney and I have visited many countries and have met some very interesting people. We thoroughly enjoyed our travels, but find the greatest joy of all in being home again with our people and friends.

"The echo of a rumor at home that I am contemplating returning to the boxing game to defend the heavyweight championship reached me in Italy. This is in no sense true, for I have permanently ended my public career. My great work now is to live quietly and simply, for this manner of living brings me most happiness."

Harold E. "Red" Grange was a different story. The "Wheaton iceman" ended his amateur years with the University of Illinois in 1925. He was carried two miles on the shoulders of students and his jersey was framed. Despite the stigma attached to professional footballers, Grange turned, saying, "The same fellows who advised me not to play professional wouldn't lend me a dollar if I were broke." There was little chance of bankruptcy happening to Grange who earned more than a million dollars in his first three years as a pro. He had an offer from the New York Giants to play three games for $40,000, but turned it down for the Chicago Bears who paid him $12,000 for his first game and $30,000 for his first game in New York. Grange was presented to President Coolidge on December 8, 1926, offered a $300,000 movie contract with Arrow Picture Corporation and treated to this extravagance by Damon Runyon: "What a football player—this man Red Grange. He is melody and symphony. He is crashing sound. He is brute force." Grange himself was a realist, if not a would-be poet like Tunney. "I do not like football well enough to play it for nothing," he remarked.

In 1919 baseball suffered a nasty public relations blow when the Chicago White Sox were indicted for throwing the World Series. It was largely due to Babe Ruth that baseball continued to hold its place in American affections in the following years. Ruth, who had been a pitcher for the Boston Red Sox, took his unique place in baseball in 1920, giving the New York Yankees much to be grateful for. In 1927 he hit sixty home runs, his all-time record, confirming what everyone had always felt about him, that he was the greatest baseball player in the world. His liquor and his women, his uncouth ways only added to the love he commanded. Of all the twenties heroes, in sports, movies and elsewhere, Babe Ruth was unquestionably the most worshiped.

FADS

The post-war period brought with it an astonishing array of ephemera, amusements, games, bits of nonsense with which a tired America entertained itself. Dancers tangoed from Santa Monica to Los Angeles. Others danced endlessly in marathons—the first contest was in March 1923. A few weeks later dancers set a record of ninety hours and ten minutes. In 1928 the Madison Square Garden contest offered a purse of $5,000. One hundred thirty-five couples entered, including Mary Promitis of Pittsburgh, who managed to dance for three weeks without any ill effects. Her secret, she revealed, was soaking her feet in brine and vinegar for three weeks before the dance. She also, unlike most contestants, never seemed to lose her grip. Others would hallucinate, fight, pass out, tremble and quiver, but not Mary. Spectators dropped in on these dances, especially to see partners keep each other awake—punching, kicking and pinching were popular methods, as were insults and smelling salts. The craze was said to have begun in England and Scotland but it took firm hold here as a contest only somewhat more civilized than a gladiatorial match.

Another kind of endurance test, equally senseless but easier on the feet, was flagpole-sitting. "Shipwreck" Kelly was the country's most famous sitter, a man who had triumphed over cities all the way from Hollywood to Union, New Jersey, and who, in 1929, spent 145 days on one pole or another. The craze caught on across the country, but especially, for some reason, in Baltimore, Maryland, where fifteen-year-old Avon Foreman sat on a pole for ten days. William F. Broening, Mayor of Baltimore, sent Foreman a congratulatory letter, after touring the city to see the twenty sitters who were perched about thanks to Foreman's example. "The grit and stamina," wrote the mayor, in what has to be one of the most unusual displays of mayoral pleasure, "evidenced by your endurance from July 20th to 30th, a period of ten days, ten hours, ten minutes and ten seconds atop of the twenty-two-foot pole in the rear of your home, shows that the old pioneer spirit of early America is being kept alive by the youth of today."

After the War, Joseph P. Babcock, representative of Standard Oil in Soochow, became interested in Mah-Jongg, a Chinese game, whose rules he simplified and set down for English players. The game became enormously popular in Shanghai and filtered back to the United States. A San Francisco entrepreneur named Hammond began importing sets, and by 1922 he had brought in $50,000 worth. Soon the demand exceeded the supply—promoters were offering free lessons and exhibitions. By 1923 Mah-Jongg sets outsold radios. Twenty different books of regulations were published indicating the complexity and fluidity of the game. People developed large and mysterious vocabularies—"Pung," they said, or "chow" while "breaking the wall" and using the "Ming box." Eddie Cantor lamented all the missing mothers in his famous song, "Since Ma Is Playing Mah-Jongg."

For those who preferred to compete with themselves, young Richard Simon and his friend Schuster decided to put together a book of crossword puzzles in 1924. The small book with a pencil attached became an overnight best seller. Tiny wrist dictionaries suddenly appeared and everybody knew the two-letter word for a printer's measure. Papers reported the story of a Pittsburgh minister who wrote out his sermon in crossword form. The Baltimore and Ohio distributed dictionaries around its trains for the convenience of passengers.

Crazes aren't particularly unusual, but the twenties was the first period in which fads were aided and abetted by the radio, which had the power of life or death over momentary enthusiasms.

Ann Gerry and Mike Gouvas, winners of the World's Championship Dance Marathon, after dancing 2832 hours.

RADIO

Dilworth's Little German Band performed regularly on radio in the late 1920s.

David Sarnoff in 1916, then the assistant manager of the Marconi Wireless Telegraph Company of America, sent a note to the general manager in which he said, "I have in mind a plan of development which would make a radio a household utility in the same sense as a piano or phonograph. The idea is to bring music into the house by wireless."

It wasn't Sarnoff, however, but Dr. Frank Conrad who developed the apparatus in 1920. That fall Westinghouse produced the first broadcasting station, KDKA in East Pittsburgh. Its first November broadcast was the returns of the Cox-Harding election. Wireless operators picked up KDKA's music and were mildly annoyed by the interference, but soon other radio stations sprang up and in two years radio had gone from an oddity to a piece of standard equipment. There were concerts, news broadcasts, church services—even some programmed especially for golfers who might otherwise go without their sermons. In 1921, when Dempsey and Carpentier fought, three announcers broadcast the match to eighty stations around the country. That fight was the first broadcast of the new Radio Corporation of America, which had been organized to challenge Westinghouse's monopoly of the waves. Westinghouse responded to the challenge by broadcasting the World Series.

Montgomery Ward started selling build-it-yourself kits with 125-foot aerials, headphones and batteries for $49.50. "It entertains . . . it fascinates . . ." read the copy. Sets cost anywhere from $50 to $700. In 1922 the nation spent $60,000,000 on radios and accessories. By 1929 that figure was $842,548,000. There was a radio in one out of three homes. RCA stock rose from 85½ in 1928 to 549 in 1929. By 1929 there were 618 stations carrying programs coast to coast.

Sets sold at historic moments such as the 1924 Democratic Convention in New York. Fifteen million people listened to the 1926 World Series. At the same time that radio techniques were advancing in sophistication the wireless still retained the fascination of black magic. In 1925 an ad for a $14.50 Crosley read, "Oh boy! There's London! Last night I had Honolulu and the night before Porto Rico. Here's where I get Rome. This Crosley sure does bring 'em in. There's nothing like a Crosley!"

Under the leadership of Hoover, the government

President Coolidge, 1924.

attempted to keep commercialism off the airwaves, but that effort failed early on. In 1922 WEAF in New York broadcast the first program sponsored by a corporation, in this case real estate. It was hardly a hard sell, the company merely mentioning its name, but it was the beginning of the end. WEAF soon recruited other sponsors, Mineralava Soap and the Metropolitan Life Insurance Company. Products became interchangeable with performers, and in some cases, radio stations. WLS in Chicago stood for "World's Largest Store" or Sears, Roebuck. Rudy Vallee and Graham McNamee stood for Fleischmann's Yeast. Goodrich sponsored the masked tenor, or Joe White, and Harry Reser's Eskimos belonged to Cliquot Club. In 1929 the government, in a last effort, tried to keep commercials off prime time and suggested that there be no commercial announcements between 7:00 and 11:00 p.m. But these were merely suggestions and went, not surprisingly, unheeded.

CALVIN COOLIDGE

In 1919 the police of Boston, Massachusetts, were earning $1,100 a year out of which they had to buy their own uniforms. Inflation was high and they went on strike on September 19. The strike, coming as it did at the height of the Red Scare, was unpopular with Massachusetts. Despite efforts by Samuel Gompers to wrest some gain out of the action, Boston Police Commissioner Curtis fired nineteen men and started to organize a new department.

The Governor of Massachusetts, son of a Vermont farmer, rallied the state and country behind him by declaring that there was "no right to strike against the public safety by anybody, anywhere, any time." Coolidge's righteous stand got him the eye of the Republican organization and made him Vice-president on the Harding ticket.

Coolidge was a sour, pinched man who looked, according to one observer, as if he had been "weaned on a pickle," and, as William Allen White wrote, as if he were "looking down his nose to locate that evil smell which seemed forever to affront him." Although Coolidge reportedly could talk his friends into a stupor, he rarely ventured more than a monosyllable in public and was, consequently, the despair of Washington hostesses. Walter Lippmann suggested that he appealed to Americans because they "feel, I think, that they are stern, ascetic and devoted to plain living because they vote for a man who is. Thus we have attained a Puritanism deluxe in which it is possible to praise the classic virtues while continuing to enjoy all the modern conveniences."

Coolidge succeeded Harding as the chief executive after his predecessor's untimely demise in August 1923, and managed to do little and say less for the duration of his term in office. He was impassive on the hot subject of the Harding scandals and resistant to any form of executive action once ensconced in office. "America's business," he announced, "is business," and he fully intended to let it mind its own. Government's "greatest duty and opportunity," he pontificated, "is not to embark on any new ventures." As the highest governmental official, Coolidge saw to it that there were no new ventures. He had no policy on Prohibition except that since it was a law it should be obeyed. When there was a Pennsylvania coal strike, he let the governor handle it. He vetoed farm relief bills and the soldier's bonus. Coolidge Prosperity bloomed as the President nurtured the business community.

During his term, Coolidge frequently found himself dressed up in Indian clothes or cowboy chaps, making public appearances at Rotarian clubs around the country. He always appeared profoundly discomfited, but felt that his duties were mostly concerned with boosting America. It was his habit to take a nap from two to four hours every working morning, in case, one supposes, a new venture should try and take him by surprise. None ever did and Coolidge finished his term a popular man.

He retired to Northampton, Massachusetts, where he labored on his autobiography, revealing the inner vacuity which his reserve had disguised. "The nation with the greatest moral power will win . . ." he wrote. "If a society lacks learning and virtue it will perish . . . There is only one form of political strategy in which I have any confidence, and that is to try to do the right thing and sometimes to be able to succeed . . . The success which is made in any walk of life is measured almost exactly by the amount of hard work that is put into it." And later, of the Depression, he had this wisdom, "We all hope it will end, but we don't see it yet."

H. L. MENCKEN

"Democracy," wrote Henry Louis Mencken, "is that system of government under which the people having 35,717,342 native-born adult whites to choose from, including thousands who are handsome and many who are wise, pick out a Coolidge to be head of the State. It is as if a hungry man, set before a banquet prepared by master cooks and covering a table an acre in area, should turn his back upon the feast and stay his stomach by catching and eating flies."

Mencken was born in Baltimore in 1880 and lived there most of his life, defending it ardently against criticism. It was one of the very few things he ever defended as he rampaged his way through American letters exposing the foibles of the country in his unrestrained, uncouth, uncorked prose. Mencken and George Jean Nathan edited *The Smart Set* from 1908 till 1923 and then *The American Mercury* until 1933. The *Mercury* carried Mencken at his most apoplectic, insulting and crochety. He was a tonic for those depressed by Babbittry and sinking under the genial, optimistic dreariness of Kiwanis, boosterism and the

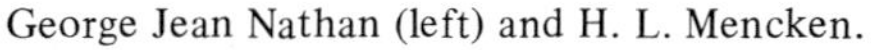

George Jean Nathan (left) and H. L. Mencken.

business of America.

Mencken wasn't having any of anything: big business, small business, big government or anarchy. "The average American of today works more than a full day in every week to support his government. It already costs him more than his pleasures and almost as much as his vices, and in another half century, no doubt, it will begin to cost as much as his necessities.

"These gross extortions and tyrannies, of course, are all practiced on the theory that they are not only unavoidable, but also laudable. . . . But that theory, I believe, begins to be quite as dishonest as the chiropractor's pretense that he pummels his patient's spine in order to cure his cancer; the actual object, obviously, is simply to cure his solvency."

Mencken was a determined and vigorous opponent of all efforts at reform. "Man is inherently vile but he is never so vile as when he is trying to disguise and deny his vileness. No prostitute was ever so costly to a community as a prowling and obscene vice crusader, or as the dubious legislator or prosecuting officer . . ."

Mencken had enemies and heroes, mostly enemies, of course, but among his heroes numbered Edgar Allan Poe, Ralph Waldo Emerson and Walt Whitman. "Let us summon from the shades the immortal soul of James Harlan, born in 1820, entered into rest in 1899. In the year 1865 this Harlan resigned from the United States Senate to enter the cabinet of Abraham Lincoln as Secretary of the Interior. One of the clerks in that department, at $600 a year, was Walt Whitman, lately emerging from three years hard service as an army nurse during the Civil War. One day, discovering that Whitman was the author of a book called *Leaves of Grass*, Harlan ordered him incontinently kicked out, and it was done forthwith. Let us remember this event and this man; he is too precious to die, let us repair, once a year, to our accustomed houses of worship and there give thanks to God that one day in 1865 brought together the greatest poet that America has ever produced and the damndest ass."

On patriotism, Mencken was predictably and deliciously perverse. "Patriotism is conceivable to a civilized man in times of stress and storm, when his country is wobbling and sore beset. His country then appeals to him as any victim of misfortune appeals to him—say, as a street-walker pursued by the police. But when it is safe, happy and prosperous it can only excite loathing. The things that make countries safe, happy and prosperous—a secure peace, an active trade, political serenity at home—are all intrinsically corrupting and disgusting. It is as impossible for a civilized man to love his country in good times as it would be for him to respect a politician."

And for those who, after all this and much more, could not understand why Mencken lived in America at all, he replied, "Why do men go to zoos?"

Willie Stevens on the witness stand. Somerville, New Jersey, November 1926.

SACCO AND VANZETTI

Nicola Sacco and Bartolomeo Vanzetti in court during their trial for murder.

A robbery in South Braintree, Massachusetts, occasioned the greatest social, intellectual and moral furor of the twenties. In April 1920, a group of gunmen executed a clumsy payroll robbery, killing two men in the process. On May 5, local police arrested Nicola Sacco and Bartolomeo Vanzetti whom they found in an interurban car. Vanzetti was found carrying shotgun shells and a loaded revolver, which later proved to belong to one of the dead men. Sacco was packing a Colt automatic and ammunition which turned out to be identical to the bullets used in the South Braintree robbery.

Sacco and Vanzetti were picked up because they were alien radicals and the United States was in the severest throes of its Red Scare. Behind every tree lurked a crazed Bolshevik, a bearded anarchist or a wild-eyed bomb thrower. Repression was the order of the day. Both Sacco and Vanzetti, who spoke very little English, were active in Boston anarchist circles. Sacco, the less articulate of the two, was a shoemaker, and Vanzetti described himself as a "poor fish peddler" from Plymouth, Massachusetts. The two men had gone to Mexico to avoid being drafted in 1916, but had fallen on hard times and had returned to the

Sacco-Vanzetti sympathizers with banners at Union Square, August 9, 1927.

United States.

Their trial was presided over by an unfriendly, right-wing judge named Thayer who had asked for the case and, out of court, talked about the "arnychists" and how he would fix them. The defendants never adequately explained their arsenal, and in light of subsequent ballistic evidence, it seems as likely as not, that they were guilty. They became, however, a cause célèbre, the liberal rallying point. Their guilt or innocence became far less important than their right to be radical in America. Judge Thayer abridged that right by giving them the death sentence.

Because the publicity surrounding the case was so great, the outcry was enormous. The Sacco-Vanzetti Defense Committee took the case out of the hands of the swaggering I.W.W. lawyer, Fred Moore, and gave it to William Thompson, a Boston lawyer, worried by the implications of the trial. He worked long and hard to get a retrial, but that decision rested with Judge Thayer who, naturally enough, refused the motion. The Massachusetts governor, Alvan Fuller, appointed an advisory committee to study the case, including Harvard's president Lowell, M.I.T.'s president Stratton, and novelist and judge Robert Grant. The committee found that it agreed with Judge Thayer, and there was no pardon. Sacco and Vanzetti were electrocuted on the night of August 22, 1927.

Vanzetti learned English during his seven years in prison and became a skillful and evocative writer. He behaved with great dignity throughout and toward the end issued a courageous statement about his political martyrdom, which many found inspirational. Both men, and particularly Vanzetti, believed that their deaths would have serious social and political meaning, which was a source of strength for them. Certainly America is no farther along on the road to an anarchist paradise than it was in 1927, but the dual execution did force the country into a profound moral crisis concerning the shape and dimensions of permissible dissent, the value of human life, and the assumption that in this democracy everything is negotiable. The finality of the execution of Nicola Sacco and Bartolomeo Vanzetti shocked liberals into acknowledging that consensus politics is frequently a myth.

LEOPOLD AND LOEB

Two nineteen-year-olds from the University of Chicago collaborated on one of the most senseless and sensational murders of the decade, if not the century. Richard Loeb, the son of a millionaire vice-president of Sears, Roebuck, and Nathan Leopold, the son of yet another millionaire, killed fourteen-year-old Bobby Franks. "Anything," they said, "is justifiable in the interests of science." Leopold elaborated, "It is no crime to use a human being in the interest of scientific research. It is not more than impaling a beetle on a pin." Loeb chimed in with one of the decade's more macabre understatements. "I'll admit we're in Dutch."

According to the young killers, they picked Bobby up on a Chicago street, struck him with a padded instrument, smothered him in a robe and stuffed a cloth in his mouth. They then proceeded to a swamp where Leopold took the stripped body to a large culvert. The two burned the boy's clothes in Loeb's furnace and buried his jewelry, shoes and belt buckle in a field in Hesseville, Indiana.

Clarence Darrow became interested in defending Loeb and Leopold because of his opposition to capital punishment. He never suggested that the two were innocent, but rather that they were too unbalanced to be held accountable for their actions. The press pilloried Darrow, his defense and the defendants, but the jury gave the pair life sentences.

Left to right: Walter Bachrach, Clarence Darrow, and Benjamin Bachrach, defense counsel at the murder trial of Leopold and Loeb (who are seated behind lawyers, Loeb partially obscured); July 24, 1924.

KU KLUX KLAN

During the twenties, the Klan, which was five years old in 1920, metastasized alarmingly. Colonel William Joseph Simmons, the Klan's founder, turned over public relations and growth to an Edward Y. Clarke who put the Klan on the map. Clarke's genius appears to have been in the area of gibberish words, Byzantine rules, self-important titles and the manipulation of rigmarole to feed the vanities and cruelties of bigots.

Clarke developed the category of Klansman known as Kleagle, naming himself Imperial Kleagle in charge of all Realms, which were, in turn, administered by King Kleagles. For the redoubtable Colonel Simmons, Clarke reserved the title Imperial Wizard, a fine tribute to the founding father. Membership in the Klan, which could only be purchased from a Kleagle, cost $10. The Klan got $6 and the Kleagle $4, which accounts for why Kleagling was such a popular trade.

In 1921, reports of some of the heinous activities of the Klan roused Congress and both Simmons and Clarke were removed from their wizardry and kleagleship respectively. Simmons was replaced by Hiram Wesley Evans, a dentist from Texas who had the curious need to refer to himself frequently and in

Ku Klux Klan parade in Washington, D.C., 1925.

President Hoover.

public as "the most average man in America." By this time, 1924, the Klan's membership had exceeded four million men. Its greatest power was concentrated in California, Ohio, Indiana, Texas, Oregon and Arkansas, but it had influence all over the country—wherever there were Americans who hated and feared Blacks, Catholics and Jews.

The Klan's objectives are best described in its own Constitution: "to unite white male persons, native-born Gentile citizens of the United States of America, who owe no allegiance of any nature to any foreign government, nation, institution, sect, ruler, person, or people; whose morals are good, whose reputations and vocations are exemplary . . . to cultivate and promote patriotism toward our Civil Government; to practice an honorable Klanishness toward each other; to exemplify a practical benevolence; to shield the sanctities of the home and the chastity of womanhood; to maintain forever white supremacy; to reach and faithfully inculcate a high spiritual philosophy through an exalted ritualism, and by a practical devotion to conserve, protect, and maintain the distinctive institutions, rights, privileges, principles, traditions and ideals of a pure Americanism." That about sums it up.

HERBERT HOOVER

Hoover, elected overwhelmingly in 1928 against the Catholic Democrat Alfred Smith, was ill-prepared to preside over the worst financial catastrophe America had ever undergone. A portly, stately man given to stiff collars and stiffer speeches, Hoover came to office with not much more imagination than Coolidge had had about what his job meant. He intended to keep government small and business big. He thought Prohibition was "a great social and economic experiment, noble in motive and far-reaching in purpose." He did not say it would work, or that he could enforce it, but he lined up with the Drys against Smith and the Wets.

Under Coolidge and Harding, Hoover had been Secretary of Commerce and as such had watched over the birth of the radio industry. In that capacity he had warned broadcasters against the deleterious effects of advertising over the airwaves. "It is inconceivable that we should allow so great a possibility of service to be drowned in advertising chatter." Two years later he continued on the same theme. "The quickest way to kill broadcasting would be to use it for direct advertising." Hoover and Al Smith each spent between $35,000 and $40,000 for radio time during their campaigns.

One of Hoover's first (and only) presidential acts was to appoint George W. Wickersham head of a committee to study the effectiveness of Prohibition and set up guidelines for its improved enforcement. The study's results were not completed until 1931 when it appeared that the country was nowhere near dry, and there was, in fact, some question as to whether it was more or less dry than it had been before the Eighteenth Amendment was passed. The eleven commissioners were divided about prospects for future enforcement. Five favored continuing things as they were. Four wanted some changes in the act, and two wanted the whole thing repealed.

In the fall of 1929, Hoover's administration was fatally wounded by the crash and subsequent downward spiral of the economy. Hoover had campaigned on lines like: "Given a chance to go forward with the policies of the last eight years, we shall soon, with the help of God, be in sight of the day when poverty will be banished from the nation." In the fall of 1929, God appeared to have withdrawn his help from the project of banishing poverty. Hoover tried at first to deny that there was any problem. "The fundamental business of the country, that is, production and distribution of commodities, is on a sound and prosperous basis." As the crisis deepened, Hoover called conferences with the leaders of big business, and they promised that wages wouldn't be lowered. The President promised a tax cut and suggested building public facilities to help ease unemployment. "I am convinced," said Hoover in his December 1929 message on the State of the Union, "that through these measures we have reestablished confidence."

Hoover spent the rest of his term predicting economic recovery or crowing over its arrival. In January 1930, the President promised economic well-being and an end to unemployment in sixty days. But prices were dropping, production was slowing down, and the market, after a brave little rally, was declining once again. Hoover tried his material once more in May, saying, ". . . we have now passed the worst and with continued unity of effort we shall rapidly recover." On the 28th he said that come autumn business would be stable. But factories were closing, stocks falling and falling, and unemployment at a record high with breadlines growing all the time.

So Hoover, who had stepped into the spot Calvin Coolidge did not choose to occupy, and who had beaten Alfred E. Smith, "the Happy Warrior," had the worst crisis of the new century on his hands with no ideas about how to handle it. He stuck by his principles—that the federal government must under no circumstances give money to American citizens lest their moral fiber be sapped. Roosevelt, as a result, cleaned up in the election of 1932, and Hoover was undoubtedly just as glad.

CRASH

Bruce Barton, founder of Batten, Barton, Durstine and Osborne, wrote the most popular book of the twenties, a book which revealed for the first time the real Jesus, a strong-willed, tough-minded, magnetic guy with great business sense. "A physical weakling!" Barton wrote with scorn. "Where did they get that idea? Jesus pushed a plane and swung an adz; He was a good carpenter. He slept outdoors and spent His days walking around His favorite lake. His muscles were so strong that when He drove the money changers out, nobody dared to oppose Him!

"A killjoy! He was the most popular dinner guest in Jerusalem! The criticism which proper people made was that He spent too much time with publicans and sinners (very good fellows, on the whole, the man thought) and enjoyed society too much. They called him a 'wine bibber and a gluttonous man.'

"A failure! He picked twelve humble men and created an organization that won the world."

Barton felt that Jesus' reputation had been tarnished over the years and needed some refurbishing and modernizing. He presented Christ as a muscular, corporate Success who had worked his way to the Top. Success in business was the twenties measure of a man, and business had never been better. Profits were up in most industries thanks to new consumer demands for items like radios, electric refrigerators and better cars. Participation in the stock market increased although it was never as widespread as myth has since had it. A million and a half investors put their money into stocks and were rewarded for their efforts. A nurse pulled down $30,000 and a butler $250,000.

The inflated conditions of the market frightened some, but most were sanguine and believed that God in His infinite wisdom intended the sun to rise in the East and the prices of stocks to rise on the Street. "We have had booms and collapses in the past. But now we have no boom. Our progress is rapid—but sure. Buying is now larger than it ever was—but it is not frenzied. The kind of emotion which brings on a boom is absent," wrote the complacent Samuel Crowther in *Colliers*.

The market, by September 1929, was ready to break from the weight of overextended buying. It did so on the 19th, but recovered itself only to slip again and recover again. Disaster struck unequivocally during the week of October 20th, when prices fell and fell, the margin collapsed and everyone was selling at devastatingly low prices. No one was willing to admit what was happening. The Harvard Economic Society stated on October 26th that, "despite its severity, we believe that the slump in stock prices will prove an intermediate movement and not the precursor of a business depression such as would entail prolonged further liquidation." Chairman of the National City Bank of New York, Charles E. Mitchell, said on October 22, "I know of nothing fundamentally wrong with the stock market or with the underlying business and credit structure. . . . The public is suffering from 'brokers' loanitis.' "

On the cataclysmic 24th of October, it seemed for a while as if there would be no bottom to the dropping prices. A little after noon of that horrendous day, Mitchell and four other bankers agreed to use $40,000,000 each to form a pool with which to come to the rescue of the market. Thomas Lamont of J. P. Morgan and Company announced to reporters unamused by his understatement, "There has been a little distress-selling on the Stock Exchange, and we have held a meeting of the heads of several financial institutions to discuss the situation. We have found that there are no houses in difficulty and reports from brokers indicate that margins are being maintained satisfactorily." Richard Whitney, vice-president of the Stock Exchange, went into the fracas on the floor of the Exchange and bought 10,000 shares of steel, and approximately twenty other stocks. This steadied pulses a bit, but had no real effect in curing what was a terminal condition. The market was having a *crise de foi* from which it would take years to recuperate.

Rumors that afternoon put suicides at eleven. In fact, the only documented death was that of the president of Union Cigar who fell or jumped from the ledge of a New York hotel when his company's stock plunged from $113.50 to $4 a share. The market continued its fall, reaching its nadir on November 13. It was, of course, the end of the Big Bull Market, the Roaring Twenties, and the beginning of the Great Depression.

Opposite page: Stock market traders watching ticker tape, 1929. *Next page*: Bessie Smith, 1923.

HITS OF THE TWENTIES

Alabamy Bound

Words by B. G. DeSylva and Bud Green
Music by Ray Henderson

C7 E♭7 Gm C7 F B♭6 A7 Dm B♭7
So I'm go-in' where there's more— Good - bye,
Of that sun-shine far a - way— Hel - lo,
Dm A Dm A Dm A Dm Gm A7 Gm A7 Dm Gm F Am7 Dm
blues Troub-les are o-ver I'll be in clo-ver soon:
joy No one's been sad-der Now I'll be glad a-while:
Chorus
B♭9 G7
I'm Al-a-bam-y Bound There'll be no "Hee-bie Jee-bies" hang-in' 'round-
mf
G9-5 C♯dim Dm
Just gave the mean-est tick-et man on earth— All I'm worth

F G7 G7-5 C7 Cdim C7
To put my toot-sies in an up-per berth
Just hear that
I'm just a
Bb9 G7
choo-choo sound
I know that soon we're goin' to cov-er ground
luck-y hound
To have some-one to put my arms a-round
G9-5 F Am7-5 D7 G7
And then I'll hol-ler so the world will know
That's why I'm shout-in' for the world to know
"Here I go"
Bb C Bb C7 F Fdim C7 F Gm7 C7 F
I'm Al-a-bam-y Bound.
I'm Al-a-
Bound.
sfz

Among My Souvenirs

Words by Edgar Leslie
Music by Horatio Nicholls

Refrain (not fast)
Eb Bbdim Fm Bb7 Bb9+ Ab Eb
There's no - thing left for me, Of days that used to be,
p-f legato
Ebdim Fm7 Bb7 Eb Bbdim
I live in mem - o - ry a - mong my sou - ven - irs. Some let - ters
Fm Bb7 Bb9+ Ab Eb Ebdim Fm7 Bb7
tied with blue, A pho - to - graph or two, I see a rose from you a -
Eb Eb7 Db Eb7 Ab Bb7 Bb9+
mong my sou - ven - irs. A few more to - kens rest with - in my
mf

Eb Bb Eb Bb7 Ab Bbdim Fm
trea - sure chest, And tho' they do their best To give me
G Cm F9 Bb7+ Eb Bbdim Fm Bb7 Bb9+
con - so - la - tion, I count them all a - part, And as the
rit.
a tempo
Ab Eb Ebdim Fm7 Bb7
tear drops start, I find a bro - ken heart a - mong my sou - ven -
1. Eb Cm7 Fm Bb7+
irs.
2. Eb Abm6 Eb
irs.
f

Are You Lonesome Tonight?

Roy Turk and Lou Handman

C F Fm C C7 F
heart? Do the chairs in your par - lor seem emp - ty and
Cm D7 G7 F♯7 G7
bare? Do you gaze at your door - step and pic - ture me there? Is your
C C7 B♭° D7 G7
heart filled with pain, Shall I come back a - gain? Tell me, dear, Are You
1. 2.
C D7-9 G7 C F Fm C
Lone - some To - night? Are You night?
rit.

The Best Things In Life Are Free

B. G. DeSylva, Lew Brown and Ray Henderson

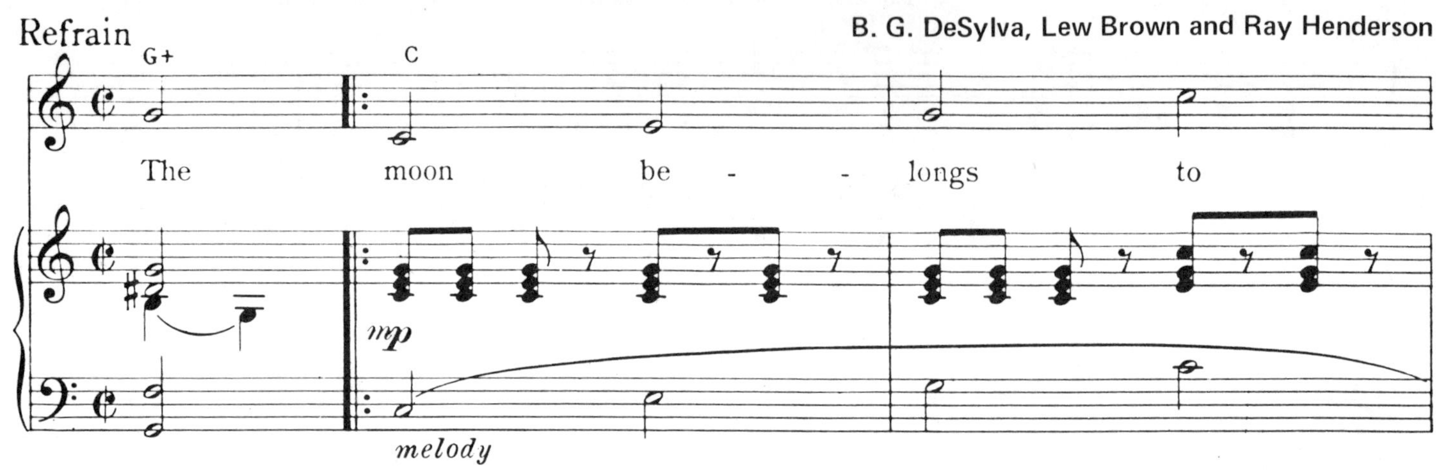

F Dm F
Bdim
long to ev - 'ry - one
They
G7
G7(♭9)
C Gdim
gleam there for you and me.
G7
C7
The flow - ers in Spring,
The
mf
F
D7
rob - ins that sing,
The sun - beams that shine

Dm7
G9
G7
They're yours, They're mine! And
rit.
p
C
Adim
Bmb6
love can come to ev - 'ry - one,
a tempo
G7(b5)
Am(b6)
Dm
C
Cdim
Dm7
G7
The best things in life are
cresc.
mf
1.
C
Cdim
Dm7
G7
free.
2.
C
Ab7
C
free.
sf

Button Up Your Overcoat

B. G. DeSylva, Lew Brown and Ray Henderson

Refrain
G Am C G Dm6 E7 A7 A7(add6)
But-ton up your o-ver-coat_ When the wind is free
But-ton up your o-ver-coat_ When the wind is free
Fdim D7 Fdim D7 G6 Cmaj7 D7
Take good_ care of your-self_ you be-long to me!
Take good_ care of your-self_ you be-long to me!
G Am C G Dm6 E7 A7 A7(add6)
Eat an ap-ple ev-'ry day;_ Get to bed by three
Wear your flan-nel un-der-wear_ When you climb a tree
Fdim D7 Fdim D7 G6 G7 Dm7 G7
Take good_ care of your-self_ you be-long to me! Be care-ful
Take good_ care of your-self_ you be-long to me! Don't sit on

C C6 C G Gmaj7 G6 Em7
cross-ing streets Oo - oo! Don't eat meats Oo - oo! Cut out sweets
hor-nets' tails Oo - oo! Or on nails Oo - oo! Or third rails
A7 D7 Em7 D9 Gmaj7 Am7 C♯7 G Am
Oo - oo! You'll get a pain and ru - in your tum-tum! Keep a-way from
Oo - oo! You'll get a pain and ru - in your tum-tum! Don't go out with
C G Dm6 E7 A7 A7(add6) Bdim D7
boot-leg hootch — When you're on a spree Take good —
col-lege boys — When you're on a spree Take good —
Bdim D7 G C7 1. G Cdim Gdim 2. G
care of your-self — you be - long to me. me. —
care of your-self — you be - long to
f
sf

Carolina Moon

Refrain

Moderately slowly and dreamily

C
G
hop - ing to - night you'll go, go to the right win - dow,
A7
Am7
D+
scat - ter your light, say I'm all right, please do.
G
C
Cm6
G
Tell her that I'm blue and lone - ly, dream - y Car - o -
1.
2.
A7
D7
G
Am7
D7
G
C
E♭7
G
lin - a moon. moon.
rall.
mf
p
Ped.

Charley, My Boy

Gus Kahn and Ted Fiorito

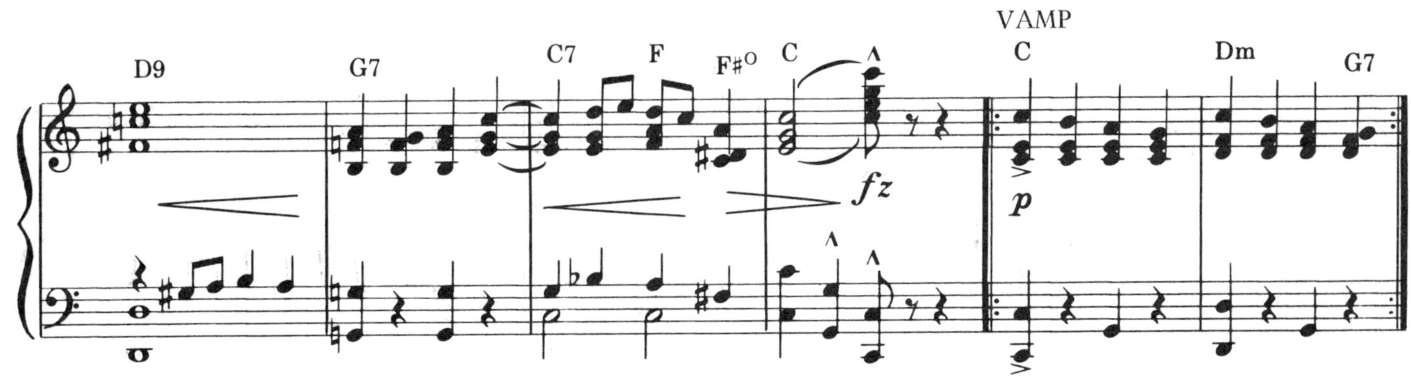

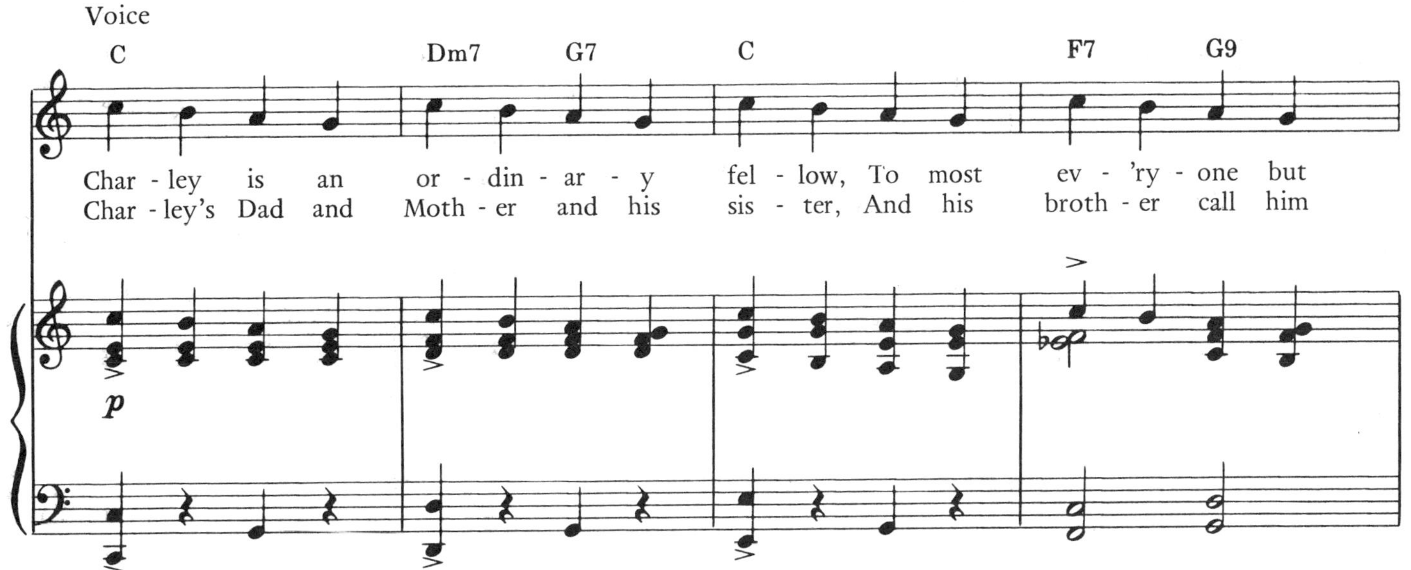

C C° C A♭9 C7 C° D∅7 C E♭°7 G7 C
Flo, his Flo. She's con-vinced that
pest, just pest. While his girl's re -
G7 C F7 G7 C C°7 C G7
Char - ley is a ver - y ex - tra - ord - in - ar - y beau, some
la - tions say if he would stay a - way we'd have some rest, some
C7 C F C7 G♯° Am B♭ F C B B♭
beau. And ev - 'ry eve - ning in the dim
rest. Her fa - ther's clean - ing up his ri -
A D D7 D G7 G7♭9
light, She has a way of put - ting him right.
fle, But she says dear - ie that's a tri - fle.

CHORUS
C
G7
Am
G7
C
Char - ley, my boy, Oh, Char - ley, my boy, You thrill me, you
Char - ley, my boy, Oh, Char - ley, my boy, You thrill me, you
p f
D7
G7
chill me, with shiv - ers of joy. You've got that kind - a sort - a
chill me, with shiv - ers of joy. You've got that kind - a sort - a
C
G7
bit of a way, That makes me, takes me, tell me what shall I say,
bit of a way, That makes me, takes me, tell me what shall I say,
C Am Em Am C
Em Am
C G7
And when we dance I read in your glance, Whole
And when we dance I read in your glance, Sweet

C7 F A♭7
pag-es and ag-es of love and ro-mance. They tell me Ro-me-o was
no-tions and o-ceans of love and ro-mance. My Moth-er told me that I
C A7 D7 G7
some lov-er too, But boy, he should have tak-en les-sons from you,
should-n't be kissed, But then your coax-ing ways are hard to re-sist,
C Am Em Am C E7 E+ A7
You seem to start where oth-ers get through,
My lips re-fuse but your eyes in-sist,
D7 G7 C 1. C E♭°7 D7 G7♭9 2. C C7 F F♯°7 C
Oh, Char-ley, my boy.
Oh, Char-ley, my boy.

Collegiate

Moe Jaffe and Nat Bonx

C7
F
C7
This is how they sing and car - ry on:
Lis - ten in 'cause this is what they say:
Chorus
F
C7
C'lle-giate, c'lle-giate Yes! we are col - le-giate Noth-ing in-te -
Al-pha Be - ta Del - ta Gam - ma The - ta Lam - da Chi O -
Har-vard Prince-ton Yale, Cor-nell, Vir - gin - ia Dart-mouth, Penn-syl -
mf-f
F
C7
F
med - jate No ma'am Trou - sers bag - gy
me - ga Phi Gam Lem - me Gim - me
van - ia Milk - - shake S'la - mi P'stra - mi
C7
F
And our clothes look rag - gy But we're rough and read - y Yea!
One - a Haf - fa Dol - lah Wear - a Ar - rah Col - lah, Low!
B'lo - ney and Spu - mo - ni Chow-mein mit Spag - het - ti Yea!

Bb Bbm F C7 F F#dim
— (Hot Dog) Gar-ters are the things we nev-er wear
— Spoken (Eureka) Sig-ma Kap-pa Tap-pa Haf-fa Keg
— (Excelsior) Bryn Mawr Vas-sar Choc-'late Frap-pés Wow
C G7 C7 F
And we have-n't an-y use for red hot flan-nels Ve-ry,
That's the Greek for all the lodg-es we be-long to Sock-er
These are all the col-le-ges that we be-long to Di-et
C7
ve-ry sel-dom in a hur-ry Nev-er ev-er
Soak-er Del-ta Hand-a Po-ker Eats at ev-'ry
Va-ries Ma-ras-chi-no Cher-ries. S. O. S. Ten
1. 2.
F C7 F
wor-ry We're Col-le-giate, Yes-sir-ree! ree!
smo-ker
Ber-ries
sfz

Does Your Mother Know You're Out, Cecelia?

Words by Herman Ruby
Music by Dave Dreyer

VOICE

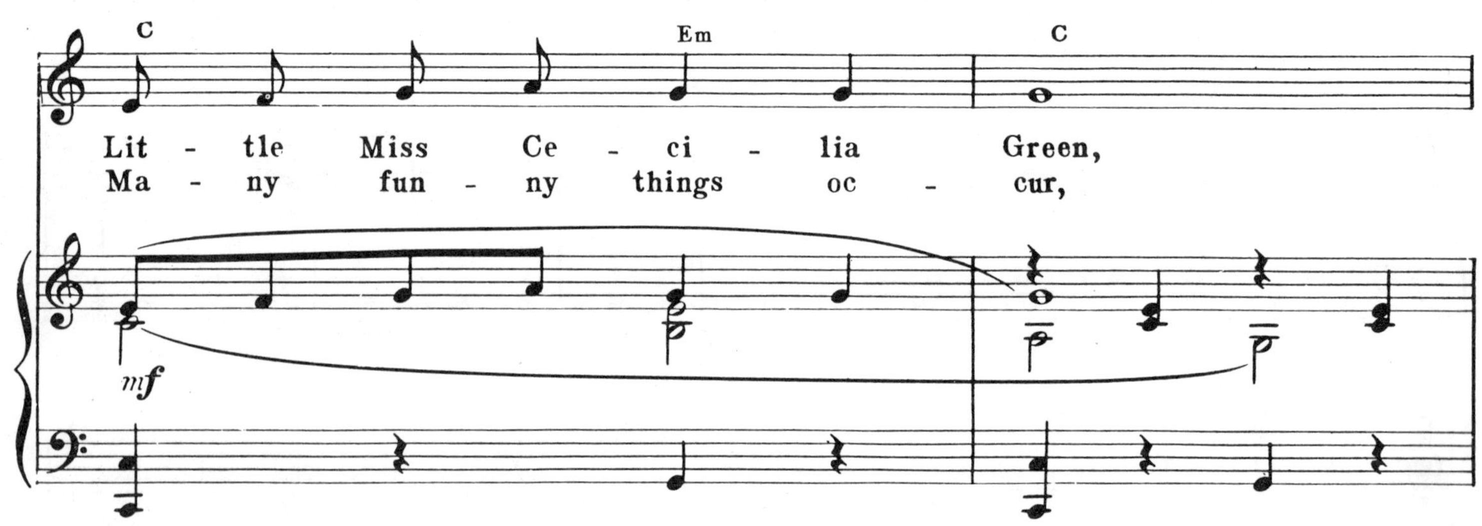

Dm
G7
Gaug
Em
Am7
But the cut - est flap - per, that you've ev - er seen
I re - fer to one case, in par - tic - u - lar
Dm7
G7
C
Em
C
When the fel - lows pass her by,
She went with a boy named Joe,
E
G#m
C#m7
Am7
D7
She will al - ways wink her eye, When she talks to them,
Who was al - ways lisp - ing so, When he'd ask this miss,
Bm
Em
Am7
D7
Dm7
G7
When she walks with them, this is what they all cry:
For a lit - tle kiss, it would sound just like this:

CHORUS
C Em Am7 Gdim Dm7 G9
Does your moth - er know you're out CE - CI - LIA?
Doeth your moth - er know you're out The - thiel - yuh?
mf-f
Dm7 G7 Dm7 Gaug Em C
Does she know that I'm a - bout to steal you,
Doeth thee know that I'm a - bout to thteal "yuh,"
Em Em7 C Cdim Dm7 Gdim G7
Oh, my, when I look in your eyes
Oh, my, when I look in your eyth
Dm7 G7 C Dm7 Cdim C G9 C Cdim G7
Some - thing tells me you and I should get to - geth - er,
I feel ve - ry you know tho un - neth - the - tha - ry,

C Em Am7 Gdim Dm7 G9
How a-bout a lit - tle kiss CE-CI - LIA,
How a-bout a lit - tle kith The-thiel - yuh,
Dm7 G7 Dm7 Gaug E9 Am Caug Am7
Just a kiss you'll nev - er miss CE - CI - LIA,
Jutht a kith you'll nev - er mith The - thiel - yuh,
D9 B Cdim Gaug C Em7 A7 Dm7 G9
Why do we two keep on wast-ing time, Oh, CE-CI-LIA,
Why do we two keep on watht-ing time, Oh, The-thiel-yuh
1. 2.
Dm7 Gaug C Ab9 Dm7 G9 C Bb C
say that you'll be mine. mine.
thay that you'll be mine. mine.

Gimme A Little Kiss, Will Ya, Huh?

Roy Turk, Jack Smith and Maceo Pinkard

G7 G dim G7
Dm7 B♭ G7 G7 (+5)
C C dim C G dim
turns him down, Comes back a - gain and hangs a - round,
G G7 C6 Cm
G B7 (♭5) E7
A7 poco rit. D7
G Cm6 G dim G7
Wait - ing for one kiss, While he pleads like this;
poco rit.
Chorus
C a tempo
G dim G7 G9 G7 G9
Boy: "GIM-ME" A LIT-TLE KISS, Will "ya," huh? What are "ya" gon - na miss,
Boy: "GIM-ME" A LIT-TLE KISS, Will "ya," huh? Must I go on like this,
Girl: "Gim-me" a lit - tle coat, Will "ya," huh? Sa - ble or mink or goat,
a tempo
p - mf
F C C (maj 7) C C (+5) F A7 Dm Dm7
Will "ya," huh? Gosh! oh gee! why do you re - fuse?
Will "ya," huh? Once a - gain a plea I'm gon - na make,
Will "ya," huh? My poor wrist is bare as it can be,

G7 G7 (+5) C C dim Dm7 G7 C Gdim
I can't see what you've got to lose, Aw, "gim-me" a lit - tle squeeze,
Tell me when do I get a break, Aw, say that you're giv - in' in,
Won't you buy a gold - en band for me? Aw, "gim-me" a lit - tle car,
3
G7 G9 G7 G9 E7 Am Am7
Will "ya," huh?_ Why do you "wan - na" make me blue? I
Will "ya," huh?_ An - y - thing that you ask I'll do. I'll
Will "ya," huh?_ That would be might - y nice of you. An
3
F6 A7 Dm A7 Dm G7(+5)
would - n't say a word if I were ask - in' for the world, But
take you for a lit - tle ride where we can be a - lone, And
aer - o - plane, a mo - tor boat, some pearls or dia - mond rings, But

C G7(+5) C C dim Dm7 G7
what's a lit - tle kiss be-tween a "fel - ler" and his girl? Aw,
once you kiss me, you will nev - er think of walk - ing home. Aw,
hon - ey if you feel you can't af - ford to buy those things, Then
C G dim G7
"GIM - ME" A LIT - TLE KISS, Will "ya," huh? And I'll
"GIM - ME" A LIT - TLE KISS, Will "ya," huh? Or I'll
"GIM - ME" A LIT - TLE KISS, Will "ya," huh? And I'll
D7 G7 G7(+5) 1,2, C Ab9 G7 G7(+5) 3. C
give it right back to you.
steal a - bout ten from you.
give it right back to you.

I Never Knew

Words by Gus Kahn
Music by Ted Fiorito

E7
Ami
But un - til I saw them all a - round you,
All my life I'm long - ing, dear to hold you,
D7
G
I was blind be - cause I nev - er knew.
Ev - 'ry sin - gle day I'll say once more.
CHORUS
G
Cmi
G
Cmi
I NEV - ER KNEW that ros - es grew, Or if
p-f
Melody
G
Ami
G
skies were blue or gray,

G
Cmi
G
I NEV - ER KNEW when breez - - es
Cmi
G
A mi
blew, What a Sum - - mer breeze could
G
B mi
say.
I NEV - ER
E mi
B mi
E mi
KNEW that dreams came true, And

Bmi
G7
C#7
F#7
Bmi
D aug.
A mi
C mi
D7
took your cares a - way,
G
C mi
G
I NEV - ER KNEW what love could
C mi
G
A mi
do, Un - til I met you to -
1.
G
D dim.
A mi
D7
day.
2.
G
day.

(I Wanna Go Where You Go—Do What You Do) Then I'll Be Happy

Words by Sidney Clare and Lew Brown
Music by Cliff Friend

F
F6
F7
HAP - PY.
If you go North or South,
If you go
F6
F7
G9
East or West,
I'll fol - low you Sweet heart
And share your
C6
C7
F
C7
Fdim
F
Fdim
B♭
F
lit - tle love nest.
I wan - na go where you go,
Fdim
B♭
F
C7
Cdim
C6
C7
C6
C7
Do what you do,
Love when you love,
THEN I'LL BE
1.
2.
F
F7
Fdim
B♭m6
F
C7
Fdim
F
F7
Fdim
B♭m6
F
HAP - PY.
I wan - na
HAP - PY.
sf

I'll Get By

Words by Roy Turk
Music by Fred E. Ahlert

G7 G9 G7 G7+5 C Em6 C♯o Dm7 G9 C6 Do C6
not com-plain, I'll see it through. Pov-er-ty
G7 C Bm7 E7 E7+5 Dm A7-9
may come to me, that's true, But
Dm7 E7+5 E7 E7-9 Am Em7 A9 A7+5 Dm7
what care I, say, I'll Get By as long as I
G7-9 1. C6 Am7 Dm7 G7 2. C6 A♭maj7 A♭6 D♭9 C6/9
have you. you.

If You Knew Susie
(Like I Know Susie)

B. G. DeSylva and Joseph Meyer

F7
this fair las - sie Oh, Oh!
nice tight dress - es Oh, Oh!

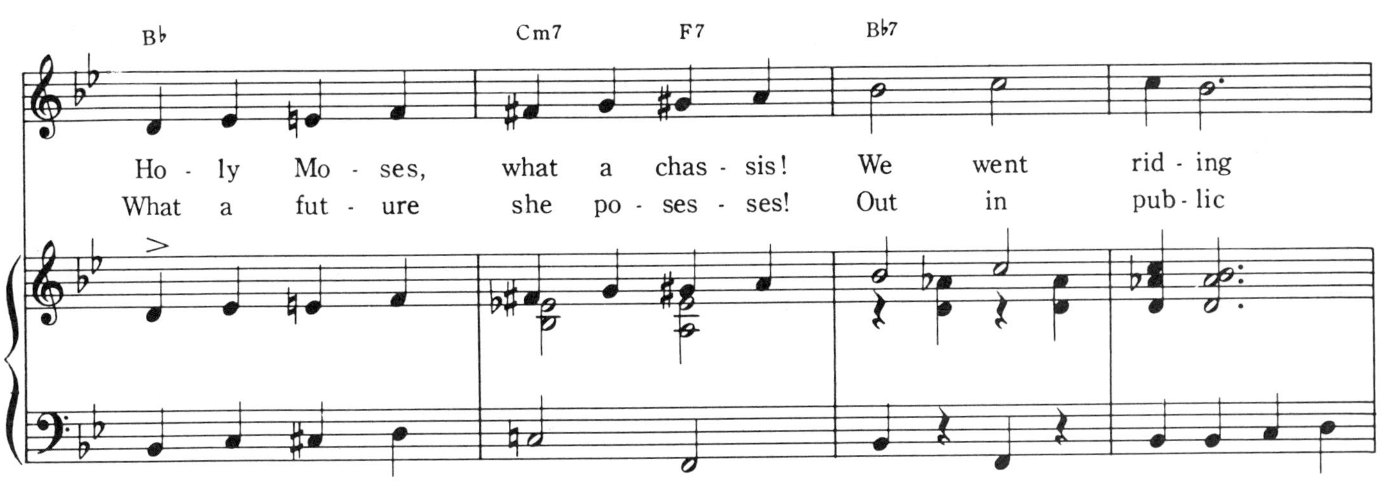
B♭ Cm7 F7 B♭7
Ho - ly Mo - ses, what a chas - sis! We went rid - ing
What a fut - ure she po - ses - ses! Out in pub - lic

E♭ B♭+ Gm7♭5 C7
She did - n't balk Back from Yon - kers
How she can yawn In a par - lor

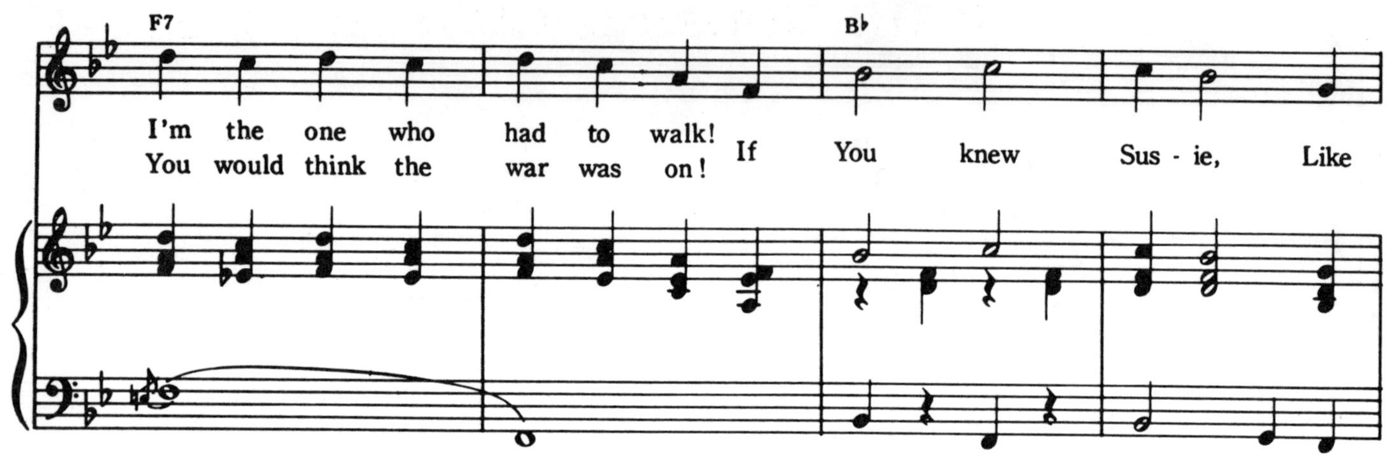
F7
B♭
I'm the one who had to walk!
You would think the war was on!
If You knew Sus - ie, Like

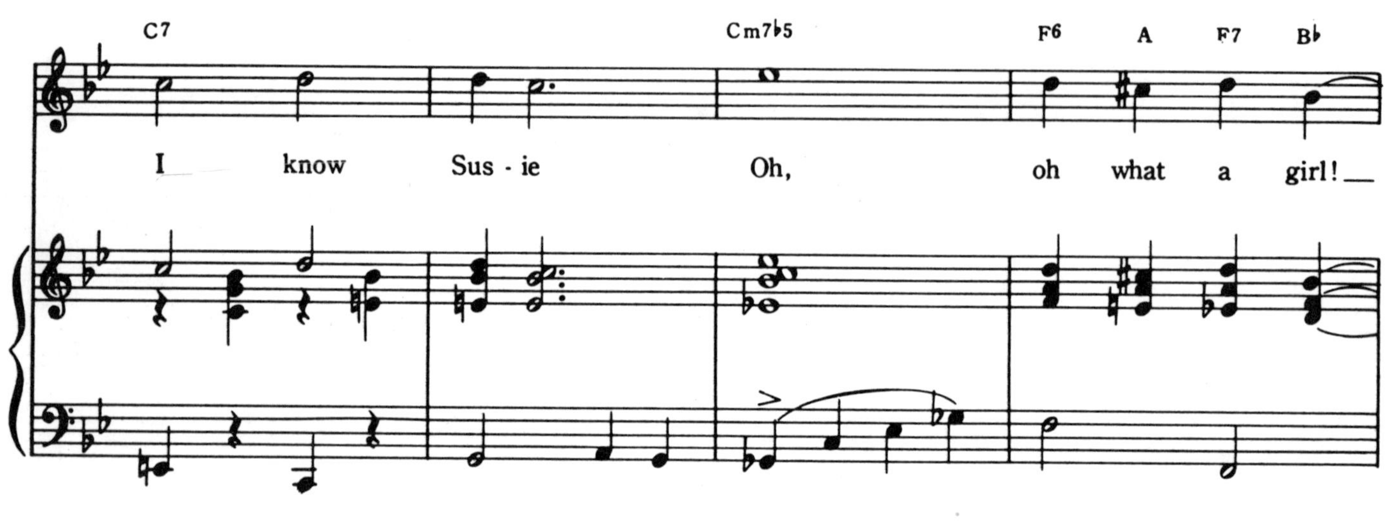
C7
Cm7♭5
F6
A
F7
B♭
I know Sus - ie Oh, oh what a girl!

1.
2.
G♭7
F7
B♭
F7♭9
B♭
If
fz

It All Depends On You

Moderato

B. G. DeSylva, Lew Brown and Ray Henderson

Dm7 G7 C Dm7 G7 G+ C6
Flow-ers de-pend on sun - shine, And the morn-ing dew.
Would-n't it make you proud, dear, If I made a name?
Dm7 G7 Am Am7 B7 Em B G7
Each thing de-pends on some-thing, And I de-pend on you.
But if I failed to win, dear, Would you want all the blame?
rit.
Refrain
C maj.7 C6 C maj.7
I can be hap - py, I can be sad, I can be good or
mp
C6 Em7 C Cdim Dm7 G7
I can be bad, It all de - pends on you.

Dm
F+
Dm7
G7
I can be lone - ly out in a crowd,
Dm
F+
Dm7
G7
G9
G+
I can be hum - ble, I can be proud, It all de - pends on
C
Cdim
C
G7
Dm7
G7
C
Cmaj.7
C7
you.
I can save mon - ey, or spend it,
mf
p
F
F6
C+
Cm6
D7
D9
Go right on liv - ing, or end it, You're to blame, hon - ey,

D7
Dm7
G7
Cdim
G7
For what I do.
I know that
L.H.
C maj.7
C6
C maj.7
Gm6
I can be beg - gar, I can be King,
I can be al - most
A7
D7
Dm7
G7
an - y old thing, It all de - pends on
mf
1.
C
Cdim
G7
G+
you.
2
C
Cdim
G7
C
you.
f
sf

Me And My Shadow

Words by Billy Rose
Music by Al Jolson and Dave Dreyer

Gmi
C7
Bb
F7
Bb C7 F9 Bb7
Pass me one by one
Guess I'll wind up like I al-ways do, with on-ly
Put their slip-pers on
They're all set but we're still on the go, so lone-ly
CHORUS
Eb
Abmi
Fmi
Me and my sha - dow
p-f
Bb7
Eb
Ab Bb7
Eb
stroll-ing down the av - en - ue
Me
D7
Cmi
Ebmi F7
and my sha - dow
not a soul to tell our trou-bles

Bb7
F7
Bb7
Eb
Eb9
Ab
to
And when it's twelve o'-clock
we climb the stair
Db7
C7
F9
Bb7
Bb aug
we nev-er knock
for no-bod-y's there
Just
Eb
Abmi
Fmi
me and my sha - dow
All a-lone and
Bb7
1
Eb
B♮9
Ab
Bb7
2
Eb
Eb7
Abmi
Eb
feel-ing blue
blue

Mean To Me

Roy Turk and Fred E. Ahlert

F maj 7 F6 Dm Dm7 G7 Gm7 C7 F Dm
cry - in'. I don't know why. I stay home
Gm7 C9 C7 Am Dm Bb Bb6 Db9
each night when you say you'll phone You don't and I'm
F maj 7 Cm6 D+ D Gm7 C7 F maj 7 F6
left a - lone Sing - in' the blues and sigh - in'.
Cm7 F7-9 Bb(sus 4) Bb F7-9 Bb
You treat me cold - ly each day in the year,

E♭9 D9+5 D7-9 Gm Gm6 E♭9 D9+5 D9 G7
— You al - ways scold me when - ev - er some - bod - y is
Gm7 C bass C9+5 F Dm Gm7 C9 C7 Am Dm
near, dear. It must be — great fun — to be mean to me, —
B♭ B♭6 B♭m7 F maj 7 F Dm7 Gm7 C9
You should - n't, for can't you see — what you mean to
1. 2.
F B♭9 G7 Gm7 C7+5 F B♭9 F
me. You're me.
3
3

My Mammy
(The Sun Shines East—The Sun Shines West)

Words by Sam Lewis and Joe Young
Music by Walter Donaldson

G7
C
day that you stray,
deep in your mind,
But wait un-til you are fur-ther a-way,
You know you just left the best pal be-hind,
Ab7
Dmi
C
G
Gaug.
C
Things won't be so love - ly,
Af - ter all our trav - els,
When you're all a - lone,
Where do we all wend?
cresc.
C
A7
G
E7
C
Cmi
D7
G
Gaug.
Here's what you'll keep say - ing,
Back home to our first love,
When you're far from home.
At the jour-ney's end.
cresc.
rall.
poco rall.

C
Emi
F
C
CHORUS Slowly with expression
Mam - - my, Mam - - my, The
p-f sostenuto
p
F C F F7 C F C D7 G7
sun shines East, the sun shines West, But I've just learned where the sun shines best.
leggiero
D dim.
E7
A7
Mam - - my, Mam - - my,
G Eb7 Ami 7 D7 G7
My heart strings are tang-led a-round Al- a - bam - - y.

p
C
C7
I'se a - com - in' sor - ry that I made you wait,
mp tranquillo
F
D7
G7
I'se a - com - in' hope and pray I'm not too late,
C
E mi
F
C
Mam - my, Mam - my, I'd walk a
F
C dim.
C
C mi
D7
G7
1. C
C dim.
G7
2. C
mil - lion miles for one of your smiles, MY MAM - MY. MY.
marc.
fz
f
sfz

Second Hand Rose

Chorus *(Moderato)*

B♭6 F+ B♭6 Gm Cm6 Gm Cm6 Gm F♯dim Gm
new ___ Ev - en Jake the plum - ber, he's the man I a - dore _
do ___ Once while stroll - ing thru the Ritz a girl got my goat _
B♭m6 F B♭m6 F B♭m6 G7 G7♭5 C7sus. C9+
_ He had the nerve to tell me he's been mar - ried be - fore _
_ She nudged her friend and said "Oh look! There's my old fur coat" _
F Fdim C7 F G7 Gm7
Ev - 'ry - one knows _ that I'm just Sec - ond Hand Rose _ From Sec - ond
Ev - 'ry - one knows _ that I'm just Sec - ond Hand Rose _ From Sec - ond
sfz
1. 2.
C7 C9 C7♭9 F Fdim C7 F Fdim Gm7♭5 F B♭ Gm7 D♭9 F6/9
Av - en - ue. I'm wear - ing
Av - en - ue. ___

Side By Side

Harry Woods

D7 Gm B♭7 E♭
sure it al - ways will That's how I feel a - bout
things we know we've got We all for - get a - bout

F7
some - one How some - bod - y feels a - bout me We're
moon - light As soon as we've giv - en our vow But

B♭ F7 B♭ B♭dim B♭7
sure we love each oth - er___ That's the way we'll al - ways be:
we'd all be so hap - py___ If we'd start and sing right now:

CHORUS
Eb
Ab
Eb
Oh! we ain't got a bar - rel of mon - ey, May - be we're rag - ged and
p-f
Ab
Eb
Ab
Eb
C7
F7
Bb7
Eb
fun - ny, But we'll trav - el a - long_ Sing-in' a song_ side by side.
Ab
Eb
Ab
Eb
Don't know what's com-in' to - mor - row, May - be it's trou - ble and sor - row, But we'll
Ab
Eb
C7
F7
Bb7
Eb
G aug
trav - el the road,_ Shar-in' our load_ side by side. Thru all kinds of

G7
C7
F7
weath - er
What if the sky should fall
Just as long as we're to -
B♭7
B♭ dim
B♭
E♭
geth - er, It does - n't mat - ter at all.
When they've all had their quar - rels and
A♭
E♭
A♭
E♭
A♭
part - ed
We'll be the same as we start - ed
Just trav - 'lin' a - long
E♭
C7
F7
B♭7
1.
E♭
2.
E♭
Sing - in' a song side by side.
Oh! we
side.
fz

Sonny Boy

Al Jolson, B. G. DeSylva,
Lew Brown and Ray Henderson

Refrain
Eb Bbm6 C7 Fm Fm7 Bb7
When there are gray skies, I don't mind the gray skies,
mp
Eb Ebdim Fm7 Bb7 Eb
You make them blue, Son - ny boy
Friends may for -
Bbm6 C7 Fm Fm7 Bb7 Cm
sake me, Let them all for - sake me, You'll pull me
Fm7 Bb7 Eb Ab7 Eb Fm G7
through, Son - ny boy.
You're sent from Heav - en And
mf

C7
F7
I know your worth; You've ma a heav - en For
B♭
E♭m6
Gdim
B♭7
E♭
B♭m6
C7
me right here on earth!
When I'm old and gray, dear,
And then the an - gels grew lone - ly,
poco rit
mf
Fm
Fm7
B♭7
E♭
Fm7
B♭7
B♭7+
Prom - ise you won't stray, dear, I love you so, Son - ny
Took you 'cause they're lone - ly, Now I'm lone - ly too, Son - ny
1.
E♭
E♭9
Fm7
B♭7
B♭7+
boy.
2.
E♭
A♭m6
E♭
boy.
sf

That Old Gang Of Mine

C7 Bb Cdim C7 F7 Fdim F7
I nev - er thought that I'd want them so bad
No - bod - y knew how I want - ed to cry
rall.
CHORUS
Bb Gdim Bb Dm7 Gm7 D7 Gm C9
Gee but I'd give the world to see THAT OLD
mf-f a tempo
C7 C9 F7 Ddim F7
GANG OF MINE I can't for-get that
Dm F7 Dm F7 Bb Gdim F7 Ddim F7 Eb F7
old quar-tette that sang "Sweet Ad - e - line" Good -

Bb7 Fm7 Bb7 Fm7 Bb7 Eb Bb7 Cdim Eb Bbm
bye for - ev - er old fel - lows and gals, Good -
C7 Gm7 C7 Gm7 C7 F7 C7 Fdim F7
bye for - ev - er old sweet-hearts and pals (God bless them)
Bb Gdim Bb Dm7 Gm7 D7 Gm C9
Gee but I'd give the world to see THAT OLD
Eb F9 Bb C9 F7 Cm F7 Bb Cm7 Bb
GANG OF MINE. MINE.
1
2.

That's My Weakness Now

Bud Green and Sam H. Stept

Gm
Eb7
Bbdim
F7
Eb7
I just had a change of heart,_ What can it be?
Guess you know the rea - son now_ Well, can't you tell?
CHORUS
Eb
Ebdim Eb
Eb
Ebdim Eb
Bbdim Bb7
She's got eyes of blue, I nev - er cared for eyes of blue, But she's got
She talks ba - by talk, I nev - er cared for ba - by talk, But she talks
p f
F+ Bb7
F7
Bb7
Eb
Eb
Ebdim Eb
eyes of blue, And that's my weak - ness now. She's got dim - pled cheeks,
ba - by talk, And that's my weak - ness now. She likes 'gage - ment rings,
Eb
Ebdim Eb
Bbdim Bb7
F+ Bb7
I nev - er cared for dim - pled cheeks, But she's got dim - pled cheeks, And
I nev - er liked en - gage - ment rings, But she likes 'gage - ment rings, And

F7 Bb7 Eb Eb7 Ab Ab7 Eb
that's my weak-ness now Oh! my Oh! me Oh! I
that's my weak-ness now Oh! yes Oh! yes And we're
Eb Cm Bbm C7 F7 F7b5 Bb7
should be good, I would be good, but gee!
head - in' for the par - son's door, I guess
Eb Ebdim Eb Eb Ebdim Eb Bbdim Bb7
She likes to bill and coo, I nev - er liked to bill and coo, But she likes to
She likes a fam - i - ly, I nev - er liked a fam - i - ly, But she likes a
1. 2.
F7 Bb7 F7 Bb7 Eb Bbdim Bb Bb7+ Eb
bill and coo, And that's my weak - ness now.
fam - i - ly, And that's my weak - ness now.
sfz

There's A Rainbow 'Round My Shoulder

Al Jolson, Billy Rose and Dave Dreyer

C G C7 D7 G Bmi
care for. I'm yell-ing, I'm tell-ing
dim-ple. I'm cheer-y, my dear-ie,
G D
folks ev-'ry-where, I know that she loves me,
an-swered my song, She said that she loves me,
A7 D Gmi Ddim. D7 Daug.
So what do I care.
How can I go wrong.
CHORUS
G Ami G Emi
THERE'S A RAIN-BOW 'ROUND MY SHOUL-DER, And a sky of blue a-
p-f

G
Emi
G
Bmi
A7
D7
bove, Oh the sun shines bright, the world's all right, 'Cause I'm in
G
C7
G
Ami
G
Emi
love. THERE'S A RAIN-BOW 'ROUND MY SHOUL-DER, And it fits me like a
G
Emi
G
Bmi
A7
D7
glove, Let it blow and storm, But I'll be warm, 'Cause I'm in
G
G7
C
love. Hal-le-lu-jah, How the folks will stare, When they see the dia-mond

Cmi
sol - i - taire, That my lit-tle su-gar ba - by, Is go - ing to
G Daug. Dmi E7
A7
D7
G
Ami
G
wear, (Yes Sir!) THERE'S A RAIN-BOW 'ROUND MY SHOUL-DER, And a
Emi
G
Emi
G
Bmi
sky of blue a - bove, And I'm shout-ing so the world will know that
1. A7
D7
G
Ddim. D7
2. A7
D7
G
I'm in love. THERE'S A love.

Together

B. G. DeSylva, Lew Brown and Ray Henderson

F
C9(sus6)
F
Dm
F
be. To - geth - er, To - geth - er, heed - less of
May. But, now in De - cem - ber, love is an
Dm6
A
E7
A
C7
weath - er, Now there is on - ly me, dear.
em - ber, 'Cause you have gone a - way, dear.
mf
rit.
Refrain
F
C7
C+
We strolled the lane, to - geth - er; Laughed at the rain, to -
p-f
L.H.
F
D7
Gm
geth - er, Sang love's re - frain, to - geth - er. And we'd
We knew
L.H.
L.H.

G7
B♭m6
rit.
F
a tempo
both pre - tend, It would nev - er end. One day we cried, to -
long a - go, That our love would grow. Through storm and sun to -
rit.
a tempo
C7
D7
Gm
geth - er, Cast love a - side to - geth - er.
geth - er, Our hearts as one to - geth - er.
L.H.
L.H.
E7
F6
C+
B+
rit.
D7+5
D7
Gm
a tempo
You're gone from me; But in my mem - o - ry, We al - ways will
mf
rit.
p a tempo
1.
Gm7
C9
F(sus9)
F
C9
C7(9♭)
2.
Gm7
C7
F(sus9)
F
be to - geth - er.
be to - geth - er.
rit.
mf

The Varsity Drag

B. G. DeSylva, Lew Brown and Ray Henderson

G7
A♭7
A7
dance. Don't think_ that I brag, I speak_ of the
L.H.
B♭7
C7
Drag. Why should a Sheik learn how_ to speak Lat-in and Greek bad-
L.H.
Fm
ly? Give him a neat mot-to_ com-plete, "Say it with feet glad-
G7
A♭7
G7
A♭7 G+ G7
ly!" First les-son right now; You'll love_ it and how-you'll love it!
L.H.

Refrain
C
Cmaj7
C7
F
Fm
Here is the Drag, See how it goes; Down on the heels, up on the toes.
p-f
C
Cdim
G7
That's the way to do the Var - si - ty Drag.
C
Cmaj7
C7
F
Fm
Hot-ter than hot, New-er than new! Mean-er than mean, Blu - er than blue,
C
Cdim
Dm7
G9
C
B7
Gets as much ap - plause as wav - ing the Flag!

E Am E Am E G7 C
You can pass man-y a class, wheth-er you're dumb or wise. If you all
mf
Fm C F C G7 C Cmaj7
an-swer the call, when your pro-fess-or cries: "Ev-'ry-bo-dy down on the heels,
p
C7 F Fm C
up on the toes, Stay af-ter school, Learn how it goes; Ev-'ry-bo-dy
Cdim G7 G+ C Edim Dm G7 C Fm C
1. 2.
do the Var-si-ty Drag." Drag."
sf

'Way Down Yonder In New Orleans

Henry Creamer and J. Turner Layton

C7 Cdim C7 C7+ F Fdim C7 Gm7 C7 Gm7 C7
E - den That's what I mean, Cre-ole ba - bies with flash-ing eyes
F Cm7 F7 B♭ F7+
Soft-ly whis-per with ten-der sighs "Stop! Oh! won't you give your la-dy fair a lit-tle
B♭ A7 A♭7 Dm7 G7 Gm7 C7 Cdim C7
smile" Stop! You bet your life you'll lin-ger there a lit-tle while
F Dm F D♭7 F F♯dim
There is Heav-en right here on earth With those beau - ti - ful queens
They've got an - gels right here on earth Wear-ing lit - tle blue jeans
'Way down yon - der in
C7 1. F F♯dim Gm7 Gdim Cdim 2. Gm7 F Dm Gm9 G♭7 F6
New Or - leans. leans.

When The Red, Red Robin Comes Bob, Bob, Bobbin' Along

Harry Woods

Em F♯Ø7 Baug. Em Em Bm
whis - tle, And blow them all a - way. What if I've been un -
morn - ing, I know the sun is bright. I keep still when I
Em B Em Bm Em
luck - y, Real - ly have - n't a thing, There's a
hear him, Sing - in' up in a tree, For the
G D♯dim. Em A7 D D7
time I al - ways feel hap - py, As hap - py as a king.
lit - tle an - gel of glad - ness, Brings hap - pi - ness to me.
CHORUS
G D7 G
When the red, red, rob - in comes bob, bob, bob - bin' a - long, a -
p - f

G G D G D7 G
long, There'll be no more sob-bin' When he starts throb-bin' his old sweet
G7 C Am Cm6 G
song, Wake up, wake up you sleep - y head, Get up, get
Em A7 D7 G♯dim.
up, get out of bed, cheer up, cheer up, the sun is red, Live, Love,
Am Em6 D7 G D7 G
laugh and be hap - py, What if I've been blue now I'm walk-in' through fields of

G
G
D7
G
flow'rs, Rain may glis - ten but still I lis - ten for hours and
G7
C
Cm
G
hours. I'm just a kid a - gain do - in' what I did a - gain sing - ing a
A7
Eb+11
G
D7
song When the red, red, rob - in comes bob, bob, bob - bin' a -
1.
G
D7
long. When the
2.
G
Daug.9
G
long.

You're The Cream In My Coffee

Fm7
Bbdim
Fm
Abm
Gm
Fm7/Eb
C9
I'm lost with-out you
You give my life its fla - vor
And just from learn - ing
Your es - ti - ma - tion of me
Gm
Gm(#7)
Gm7
C9
Fm6
F7
Ab/Bb
Bb7
What sug - ar does for tea
That's what you do for me
And as for you, I'll say
I feel the self same way
CHORUS
Eb
Ebdim
Fm6
Bb7
You're the cream_ in my cof - fee
You're the salt_ in my
You're the cream_ in my cof - fee
You're the salt_ in my
p-f
Fm6
stew
You will al - ways be
my ne - ces - si - ty
stew
You will al - ways be
my ne - ces - si - ty
R.H.

E♭
A♭9
Fm7
E♭dim
I'd be lost_with-out you. You're the starch in my col - lar
I'd be lost_with-out you. You're the starch in my col - lar
Fm6
You're the lace_ in my shoe You will al - ways be
You're the lace_ in my shoe You will al - ways be
E♭
F♯dim
B♭7/F
my ne - ces - si - ty I'd be lost_ with - out you.
my ne - ces - si - ty I'd be lost_ with - out you.
R.H.
E♭9
A♭add 9
Most men_ tell love - tales_ And each_ phrase dove - tails_
You give_ life sav - or___ Bring out_ its fla - vor___
cresc.

F7(6)
Fm7
F7(♭5)
You've heard each known way This way is
So this is clear, dear, You're my Wor-
B♭7/F
B♭7+
E♭6 add 9
E♭dim
my own way You're the sail of my love - boat
- cester - shire, dear, You're the sail of my love boat
Fm7(6)
You're the cap - tain and crew You will al - ways be
You're the cap - tain and crew You will al - ways be
E♭
D7
B♭7
E♭
my nec - es - si - ty I'd be lost with-out you. you.
my nec - es - si - ty I'd be lost with-out you. you.
R.H.

BRING IT ALL BACK WITH SONG

Everybody's Favorite Songs. A lively collection of 200 best loved song favorites—children's songs, patriotic, college, operatic, and sacred. Also, the folk songs of Russia, Spain and the U.S.A. With piano accompaniment. A handy chart is provided listing a variety of instruments to accompany the songs. Complete with chord diagrams.
$3.95
Order no: 020001

Treasury of Popular Classics. More than 108 celebrated melodies by the famous composers simply and effectively arranged.
$3.95
Order no: 020096

Classical Themes for People Who Hate Classical Music. The world's most often sung and played themes in simplified form. Over 100 of the world's greatest melodies, from radio, television, and the concert stage in effective, easy-to-play arrangements.
$3.95
Order no: 020100

The Great Atlantic & Pacific Song Book. Songs representing the best of American folk music. Contains words and music, guitar and banjo chords. Compiled and edited by Irwin Silber, editor of *Sing Out,* the national folk song magazine.
$3.95
Order no: 020127

Available at your local music store or directly from Music Sales Corporation, 33 West 60th Street, New York 10023. Please add 50¢ postage and handling. Write for FREE catalog.